STRIKE UP THE BAND

Two centuries of music in Dunstable and District

Anthony J. Ward

The
Book
Castle

Strike Up The Band
is dedicated to my late parents and family, without whose interest in music, early support and participation in musical activities, my own musical interests would not have flourished, and this book would never have been written.

First published June 2003 by
The Book Castle
12 Church Street
Dunstable
Bedfordshire LU5 4RU

ISBN 1 903747 22 8

Designed and typeset by Caroline and Roger Hillier
The Old Chapel Graphic Design

Printed by Print Solutions Partnership,
Wallington, Surrey

Contents

BRASS BANDS

Contents continued

ORCHESTRAS, DANCE BANDS AND THE JAZZ SCENE

DUNSTABLE CELEBRATIONS 1963

DUNSTABLE UPPER SCHOOLS BANDS AND ORCHESTRAS

Foreword

As an amateur enthusiast for history and music, and with my past family links with the Excelsior Silver Prize Band, the Bible Class Orchestra, and in other areas of music, I decided about four years ago to start a scrap book – which soon became a much wider Project. Then a friend produced some word processing for me, and that led in turn to my acquiring my own computer, and to an ever broadening area of research, eventually leading to the distillation of this material into the form of a book.

While the Project overall encompasses a broader history of music, sounds and activities in Dunstable and district, the present Book concentrates mostly on the Brass Bands, Orchestras, and similar groups from the mid-nineteenth century up until today, together with the part they have played and continue to play in the life of the town and district. The histories of choirs, bell-ringing, and various other activities have not been particularly featured however. The Project itself will continue nevertheless, and any further information, memorabilia etc will be welcomed.

I hope you will enjoy reading 'Strike up the Band'.

A. J. Ward
Dunstable, 2003

About the Author

The Author is both a resident and native of Dunstable. A member of a musical family, he recalls playing the piano from an early age and his regard for the instrument is somewhat affected by the fact that as a child in World War II, he and his family used to hide behind it during the early air raids.

He attended what was then Burr Street (now Icknield) School, was a member of the Priory choir for about four years, was taught the piano by Fred Taylor, and attended the former Dunstable Grammar school where he says they were constantly reminded of what was expected of them and that 'other schools were better than they were at woodwork and history'. In the middle 1950s he became involved with jazz, learnt the clarinet and saxophone and with a group of friends formed a jazz band, calling themselves the 'Wayfarers', the successors of which still play in the Dunstable area.

After retiring from a career as a Chartered Management Accountant in local government, he eventually started his project on the subject of local musical history. He has always been a keen sportsman, playing some local cricket for NALGO (as was), amongst other things, and still plays badminton and tennis, using, he says, 'all his experience to avoid excessive movement on court!'

His memory of two of his late uncles who were members of the Excelsior Silver Prize Band and the Bible Class Orchestra at the Square respectively was the spur to research into those organisations and others in the district, reaching as far back into history as available records and the recollections of veterans and their successors would allow, starting as a scrap book and evolving into a computer based archive from which this book is derived.

The project became a consuming interest for three years or more – time now he says for a bit of a break and to 'plan some gardening'.

Acknowledgements

I am indebted to many people who have made vital contributions to the material in these pages. In particular I must thank Mr. Douglas Darby, who has been a mine of information on a whole range of topics, in particular the Bible Class Orchestra: the Excelsior Silver Prize band: Operatic & other Societies: the inter-war years: the Pageant of Dunstable and others. Also Mr. Jim Bull, who with Mrs. Mary Dolman and Mrs. Louie Dolman contributed so much to the 'Excelsior' chapter in particular; and Mrs. Jane Stanley, for her contribution to the Franklin family, the Volunteers and the Borough Brass Band; and Mr. John Buckledee, editor of the 'Dunstable Gazette' and the 'Luton News' for kindly giving permission for newspaper pictures and material to be included.

I am also grateful to Mrs. Margaret Thompson for contributing a good deal of the earlier word processing, to Mrs. Pat Lovering for her advice and encouragement, to Paul Bowes for supporting the project and his useful suggestions and good offices particularly with respect to the expansion of the section on schools music and for publishing the book; and to many other persons referred to elsewhere.

The book is particularly built around photographs, memorabilia, and the reminiscences of those who have contributed material for the project. In most cases I think we have been able to acknowledge each contributor either in the text or as initials attached to the pictures. In some instances, individual photos have been provided by more than one person and attribution has sometimes been difficult, but it is hoped where there may be some uncertainty or error that our good intent will be accepted.

Many of the earlier photos bear testimony to the tremendous contribution to any local history of the late Mr. Charles Smy, a well known photographer in Dunstable in the past, who also has the distinction of providing the author's late parents with an early photo of the author at about the age of twelve months or so! Certain items may also have appeared in other publications on occasions where the contributor has submitted the same items for use in different topics. The list of acknowledgements on the next page is intended to include all those whose work may be included in, contributed to, or influenced 'Strike Up The Band.'

From time to time, the Book Castle reproduces historic publications that local authors will have drawn upon, often from dog-eared originals in various people's possession. One such example is the 'Dunstaplelogia' a history series

Acknowledgements continued

published in the 19th century by local schoolmaster Mr. Charles Lamborn. The author was able to use material from one or two of the originals in the collection of Mrs. J. Stanley, in the chapter on the 19th century. A complete compendium of all the separate booklets in that series was published in the autumn of 2002 by the Book Castle.

'Strike Up The Band' does not purport to be an encyclopaedia of all bands and orchestras in Dunstable and district, the main emphasis having been on the brass bands and orchestras in the immediate area. In some cases a few examples only may have been included to illustrate certain areas of music making, such as the chapters on cadet bands – and dance & jazz bands, which do not particularly include Luton and its wide history of dance bands.

The intention however, has been to entertain, and to provide historical information about music making in Dunstable and district – to pay tribute to all the participants over the years and to all those local writers and others whose work has added to the scope of material covered by the book. It is hoped that readers will be able to add to our reservoir of knowledge from time to time. Any written comments, corrections or additional information would be welcome at the publisher's address, at the Book Castle, Dunstable.

A. J. Ward
Dunstable, Winter 2002

Index to Acknowledgements

Initials	Name	Main Subject areas
MD	Mary Dolman	The Excelsior Band & others.
LD	Louie Dolman	The Excelsior Band
JD	Jaquie Dolman	The Excelsior Band
BC	Brian Cassidy	Rifle Volunteers
JG	Joyce Godber	History of Bedfordshire
MM	Maurice Matthews	WWI: & others. Queensway Hall (project)
JB	Jim Bull	The Excelsior Band, Dance Bands, BCO, etc
BT	Betty Tarbox	Kensworth Band
TE	Trevor Evans	Kensworth Band
JS	Jane Stanley	Borough Band: Franklins
OR	Omer Roucoux	John Dunstaple (project)
RW	Richard Walden	Queensway Hall (project)
BH	Beryl Hyde	Toddington Town Band
PD	Phyllida Driver	Manshead School
JM	Jonathan Mardlin	Northfields School
FT	Fred Thomas	Queensbury School
DBG	Dunstable (Borough) Gazette	Comprehensive range of photos etc
DC	Dunstable Chronicle	19th Century reports
PH	Paul Heley	The Excelsior Band, Wayfarers Jazz
AW	Tony Ward (Author)	Pageant, Other
CS	Charles Smy	Photos of early-mid 20th C.
VE	Vivienne Evans	Historical Data over a wide range (project)
PK	Pauline Keen	Moore's Shop, High St. South
WGS	Worthington G. Smith	Historical references
AF	Alec Fowler	Dunstable Priory Church & Pageant
PL	Pat Lovering	Houghton Regis & other matters
JT	James Tibbett	Editor Dunstable Chronicle 19th C.
WD	William Derbyshire	Author 19th C. History of Dunstable
BB	British Bandsman	History of Brass Bands (Arthur M. Taylor)
PMY	Percy M. Young	A History of British Music
DJ	David Janes	The Excelsior Band: Fred Janes Band
HCM	H.C. Moreton	Photos in 1919 Peace Booklet
PB	Pat Bird	Orchestras
RJ	Ray Jackson	The Salvation Army
PF	Peter Farmer	The Heath Band
MT	Margaret Thompson	Word processing early material & Gt. Brickhill
IMS	Ian M. Smith	Toddington Town Band
JC	Julia Crask	The Luton Band
JB	John Buckledee	Editor Dunstable Gazette, Luton News etc
CL	Charles Lamborn	Author Dunstaplelogia
DTC	Dunstable Town Council	Town Guides, Photo 2000 etc
DD	Douglas Darby	Bible Class Orchestra, other Orchestras, The Excelsior Band, Operatic & other societies, Inter war years, Pageant etc
FL	Fodens Ltd	Mortimer family Brass Bands
SB	Sid Bates	Gt. Brickhill Band
VL	Vauxhall Ltd	Northfields School Band

Bibliography

A History of British Music, Percy M. Young, Ernest Benn Ltd

Brass Bands, Arthur R. Taylor, Hart Davis Macgibbon

History of Bedfordshire, Joyce Godber, Bedfordshire County Council

Other sources including Dunstable Library, Bedfordshire County Council and The Book Castle publications.

Services

DPI – Dormans Photo Imaging Ltd. Broadwalk, Dunstable
for computer enhancements etc. of some of the early, damaged photos

1 THE DEVELOPMENT OF THE BRASS BAND MOVEMENT IN BRITAIN

The First Brass Band

Before 1790 there seems to have been little in the way of recorded documentation of music, bands and orchestras, either locally in Dunstable or generally for the whole country; after that however, more detail becomes available.

The North and the Midlands have always been associated with the core of the Brass Band movement, especially the Manchester area, and among the contenders for the 'first brass band' was the 'Clegg Family Band', (later called 'Besses o' the Barn', the name of the small village on the then outskirts of Manchester in which they played). It was said to have started in c.1790 as a string band, becoming a reed band in about 1818, then a brass or wind band about 1821, before later specialising in brass instruments only.

'Besses' band won a prize at a hastily introduced contest of local (Manchester) bands, celebrating the coronation of George IV in 1821. (Contests were to become a regular feature of the brass band scene). Another famous band at this time was the 'Black Dyke Mills Band' – a name familiar to most people, and still at the top of their class today.

Early Influences

There were probably four main lines of influence in the development of brass bands at the end of the 18th and beginning of the 19th centuries, namely:
>   1. *The Church Bands.*
>   2. *The City 'Waits' – official municipal musicians playing pipes, horns and drums – who heralded special occasions such as royal visits, fairs, etc. (probably defunct by 1835).*
>   3. *Military Bands – particularly active in the Napoleonic wars.*
>   4. *Rifle Volunteers.*

The 'Waits' and military bands, together with the Rifle Volunteers, all generally wore a military-style uniform of some kind.

This influence has continued until today when many bands wear uniforms as part of their image – indeed it would be rather unusual nowadays to come across a Brass Band not wearing a uniform.

Instrumentation

Many late 18th and early 19th century bands were in fact more generalised 'wind bands' which were a mixed bag of:
>   a. *Conventional brass instruments*
>   b. *Earlier brass instruments, now defunct, such as the keyed bugle, and serpent.*
>   c. *Reeds, bassoons and oboes.*
>   d. *Flutes and fifes etc.*
>   e. *A group of percussion instruments.*
>   f. *String instruments at various times.*

The early northern small town bands were often sponsored by a particular individual family or business, (as per the Clegg family above), and from these beginnings around 1818, specialised brass ensembles began to evolve. This led to the development of the nationwide and worldwide movement that still flourishes today.

The Military Dimension

Before 1818, and for a long period, military bands (bands recruited by the regular army, to support it in war and peace, and sometimes required to lead it into battle!) were to be seen and heard in various localities, comprising similar groups of instruments as described above. The modern military band in fact combines both brass, reeds (saxes, clarinets) and flutes (piccolos) and percussion, in contrast to the now traditional, more specialist brass band. Another factor was the emergence of groups of local (Rifle) Volunteers, founded during the Napoleonic wars of 1798-1815. The battalions formed bands akin to the above, and were a sort of Territorial Army of the day. They generally remained local organisations, sponsoring many local musicians in their ranks.

At the end of the Napoleonic wars, a surfeit of military ensembles remained after disbandment of the non regular units and Volunteers. Later in the 19th century (1859), the Volunteers were re-instituted when France again began pursuing anti-British policies. Dunstable was noted for its response to the movement, and it was from this second phase of Volunteers, and its Band, that the Dunstable Borough Band emerged. Both Bands existed in parallel for many years. However the Dunstable Chronicle, (founded 1855), frequently refers to 'The Dunstable Brass Band' in its reports, i.e. well before the Volunteers of 1859, the inference being that such a band could have been in existence for some time before 1855.

We can see that by about 1818 there was plenty to choose from in determining the nationwide antecedents of the Brass Band. Whatever the case for each strand of influence, bands specialising in the increasingly modernised valved instruments were becoming well established around 1821, when the first known Brass Band contest with prizes was instituted.

Militia Bands

There is little or no indication of the musical standards of the Militia bands, regular or volunteer, and no apparent uniformity in the numbers of the instrumental line-up. (Some of these bands in fact were civilians, often hired by officers under a form of contract!) Some historians state that these bands matched the standard of their Continental allies (and the defeated Napoleonic bands) – but there is a record of one British officer, from the Peninsular War, who marched through Paris with the victorious allied armies and their bands, and stated he was ashamed of the standard of the British bands, particularly in comparison to the French!

The existence of military bands in Britain, in which many of the men had been regular or volunteer soldiers (together with improving social conditions, allowing more public recreation), contributed to the expanding number of specialised civilian brass bands. By the middle of the century, brass bands were becoming a strong feature of British life, and were more and more involved in local and national events. They played a strong role in the celebration of these events from the mid-19th c. to the 1960s and after, as will be seen in chapters featuring the individual bands.

The coming of the railways from 1838 and the Great Exhibition of 1851, when ordinary people were able to afford the low rail fares, were also to play a significant part in the widening of the Brass Band movement.

Instrumental Development

Before 1815, however, most brass instruments were hampered by their design shortcomings – 1815 is a pivotal date in the development of the modern valved or piston configured instrument, allowing ease of performance, with chromatic capability – i.e. changes of key without having to substitute differing lengths of internal tubing in order to change key. The euphonium, a four valved instrument, was introduced later in 1843. However, earlier types of keyed bugles, opheclides (a sort of keyed euphonium) and rotary-pistoned cornets etc. were still being played until quite late in the mid-19th century.

The Mortimer Family

It is widely accepted that the high standards of musicianship that are now taken for granted might not have developed had it not been for the Mortimer family. Fred Mortimer senior, (who originally came from Yorkshire) and his family were very active with the 'Luton (Red Cross) Band' in the 'twenties.

Fred conducted the Luton band when it won the Crystal Palace trophy in 1923, with his son Harry at 21 taking a leading role on cornet (having recorded his first solo on cornet in 1919). Harry had also been conductor of the Luton Junior Band at 14, starting on cornet at 7 years of age.

However, the whole family was to move north about two years later in 1925 when another son Alex was persuaded to join the Foden Band on euphonium, with Harry also joining the band. Fred took over the Foden baton in 1929. Another son Rex also became a noted performer.

(FL)

The Mortimers in 1951, Fred seated, with (L–R) Alex, Harry & Rex.

Harry had also appeared in Dunstable in the 1930s Choral Union events in the town, coming as a guest trumpet soloist from the Halle Orchestra which he had joined in 1926! In 1942 Harry joined the BBC, in charge of the broadcasting of brass bands, becoming a household name for many years and bringing brass band music into academic respectability. His links with Luton & Dunstable were never forgotten.

Contests

Although various individual contests had been held from time to time, the first broadly based contest is generally accepted as having been held in 1853 at Belle Vue, Manchester, with the first to be held in the south of England being in 1860 at the Crystal Palace, London. These events gradually evolved into the National Brass Band Championships which were to take place at the Royal Albert Hall.

The Contest has played a major part in the development of standards of brass bands, becoming a widespread phenomenon all over the country in the earlier part of the twentieth century – including Dunstable, Luton and Aylesbury.

Many local and national contests are still being held at the beginning of the third millennium and the standard continues to be very high.

Percussion Instruments

Later in the century, when the American Civil War ended in 1865, a glut of band instruments, including drums (many acquired by slaves newly freed), is often assumed to have led to the emergence and development of the now traditional drum kit.

In time, various combinations of drums – and cymbals and other percussion – would become configured as a single drum kit, playable seated in situ by one individual in a brass or dance band, when no longer required to march, (except of course in the case of marching bands as such, where drums would still be played by more than one person according to the size and type of band).

Dunstable's Bands

All these influences, and others, formed the background from which Dunstable's Brass Bands: the Volunteers Band – the Dunstable Borough Brass Band – and, sponsored by a growing temperance movement, the Dunstable Temperance Band (later to become the Excelsior Band) – emerged, and later on of course the Salvation Army.

For most of the period from 1860 to 1940, Dunstable had the four bands mentioned above. However by 1940 the Borough Band had been wound up, and by the end of 1960 the Excelsior had been disbanded. The Volunteers had lasted from 1859 to 1908, when they were merged with the Territorial Army. The Salvation Army Band is still going strong in 2003 after its founding in Dunstable in about 1885. Their individual stories and those of others in the district are described in the following chapters.

The chapter on the development of the brass band movement, and the chapter on the 19th century, both take a look back into the past and attempt to assess the atmosphere and circumstances of the times, from which Dunstable's various bands emerged. We should remember too, that in 1860 the total population of the town of Dunstable was approximately 4,400, fewer than half

HOW BRASS INSTRUMENTS DEVELOPED OVER 100 YEARS OR SO

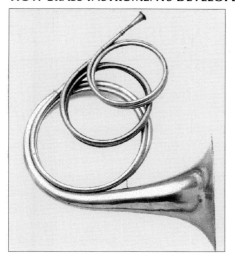

(JB)

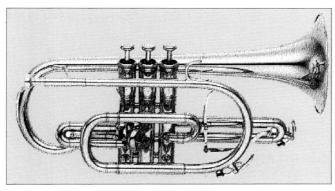

Above left: Earlier coiled instruments had a detachable series of tubes or crooks to vary the range of notes playable.

Above: A vintage model of the 'Butler Piston Cornet' or 'Vibrating Horn' with tuning crooks – a sort of halfway point between the examples above left and left.

Left: A modern cornet from a recent instrument catalogue, with slide 'triggers' fitted for improved intonation.

being males. Universal education was still to come, and the geographical area of the town was much smaller. Dunstable, in parts, was more or less indistinguishable as a separate area from Upper Houghton Regis, and in 1907 much of Upper Houghton Regis was 'ceded to Dunstable', with further boundary adjustments in 1933. The combined area was referred to in the bid for Dunstable's charter of 1864.

Houghton Regis has since remained a separate entity, and today has its own Town Council and Mayor. It also had its own brass band in the past, combining for a while with the Dunstable Temperance (Excelsior) Band. Little more is known at the time of writing however, and more research is needed.

The following pages look in greater detail at events in Dunstable and district from the mid 19th century, with some of the influences of the times, the development of the area, and the founding of the brass bands. The Bible Class Orchestra at the Wesleyan Church, the Square, also emerged somewhat later, in 1895, and its story is told in the chapter devoted to that orchestra. Other orchestras developed from the early 20th century onwards.

Later, the senior schools became the inheritors of the earlier bands and orchestras (although they generally do not march), and they can be seen and heard in the summer band season concerts in Grove House Gardens and elsewhere, together with the enduring Salvation Army Band.

2 19TH CENTURY REPORTS FEATURING LOCAL BANDS & MUSIC

The 19th Century – (Wm. Tibbett/C. Lamborn/W. H. Derbyshire)

The Battle of Inkerman 5th November 1855

Few towns made such a loyal demonstration as Dunstable in 1855 on the 5th of November, to celebrate the great and glorious battle of Inkerman. Early in the morning the Free Boys of Chew's school began to assemble, and at nine o'clock the boys sallied out of the Sugar Loaf yard, with the effigies of the Emperor and Guy Fawkes, the figure of the Emperor wearing a real trophy from the Battle of Inkerman, which was made a present by Mr James McMillan, of the Scots Fusilier Guards. After they had paraded the town they returned to the starting place to count out the proceeds, which amounted to 3s. 6d. per boy, after paying the expenses. In the afternoon, they set to work to take the fuel to the Downs, kindly granted by Lady Alford for this pleasing demonstration. In the evening, at six, the band assembled together and a procession formed in the following order:

A MAN CARRYING A NAPTHA LAMP, IN FRONT
TWO BOYS CARRYING FLAGS
BAND
'THE EMPEROR'
FIELD-MARSHALL PLUMMER
BRIGADIER JARDINE
BRIGADIER DERBYSHIRE–WITH DRAWN SWORDS
A ROW OF THE BEDFORD MILITIA
ANOTHER NAPTHA LAMP

After parading the town, they proceeded to the Downs to burn the effigy. The bonfire was a splendid sight, and with the fireworks was a grand spectacle. Upwards of three thousand people assembled on the downs.

This Chapter features references from the following sources relating to the 19th Century:

(1) The 'Dunstaplelogia' a series of historical booklets by Charles Lamborn, a local teacher and historian, published in the latter part of the 19th century – with thanks to Mrs. J. Stanley who was able to provide the author with several original copies for the project. (Now published as a whole by the Book Castle 2002.)

(2) W. Derbyshire's 'History of Dunstable' of 1872 (2nd edition) also published around the same period, per an original copy in the author's possession, and

(3) 'The Dunstable Chronicle', Dunstable's first local Newspaper published by James Tibbett from 1855 to 1859.

Note –The format of 'The Dunstable Chronicle' at this time was similar to others in the country. In 1855, the first Issue was published after the government had removed the stamp duty on newsprint. This led to a great increase in the publication of local journals. The format was: (a) Title sheet with local reports and adverts. (b) National news and adverts. (c) Full page of general adverts. (d) Reports of international events and articles. (e) Letters to the editor re. local national and international issues.

The Editor of the paper, Mr. Tibbett, was a well known figure in Dunstable. He was also secretary of the Bible Society and a strong Temperance advocate.

Although presented in the rather formal style of the times, they show how Dunstable and its citizens celebrated various events with music and pageantry, providing a flavour of the times with reports of a wide range of local cultural activities.

This chapter leads to the more detailed accounts of the brass bands established in the later part of the 1800s, as set out in the following chapters.

The End
of The War
with Russia
Summer
Solstice
24th June
1856

From a very early period the summer solstice was celebrated in the country with peculiar ceremonies, among which the kindling of fires formed a conspicuous figure. These were called bonfires*, and were a sign of goodwill among neighbours. They were a part of the heathen customs, which celebrated the summer solstice. They were intended to honour the feast of St. John the Baptist, and were regarded as being conducive to health. They were chosen as the place where old quarrels might be made up and new friendships formed.

Of all the days in the calendar, that of St. John had the greatest claim as the one on which the peace rejoicings should be held, and following the war with Russia in 1856, a more true English holiday was never celebrated anywhere, than was on this day by the loyal inhabitants of Dunstable. The first commencement of the day was the firing of a salute of twenty-one guns, in honour of the occasion. About six o'clock, a.m., the *Dunstable Brass Band* aroused the inhabitants with their music, as they paraded the town. Their performance drew forth the warmest praise from all who heard them. The bells of the ancient Priory church added their music and gave forth a merry peal. Flag after flag continued to make their appearance from all the principal houses. About ten o'clock the splendid *Band of the Bedfordshire Militia* arrived and paraded the town, headed by the Free boys carrying flags and banners. Upon the arrival of the train came the *London Band*, who marched up the town, headed by the parish beadle and Free-school boys.

On the Square, all was bustle in preparing the dinner for 1000 people; and about eleven o'clock the different districts began to assemble at the places appointed for them to meet. All were soon in readiness to march to the Square, where every arrangement was made to receive them. Around the outside of the table were flags, of various descriptions; and at the grand entrance were placed some fashionable straw hats and bonnets, in commemoration of the staple trade of the town.

At a quarter before one, the bands took their places allotted to them, and the people began to arrive for dinner; and a thousand more orderly and respectable people could nowhere be found. The sight of the Square was now one of the most splendid ever seen in Dunstable. Ample justice having been done to the real old English fare of beef and plum-pudding, the bugle horn sounded for silence, after which the band again played the Old Hundredth psalm tune, and the company returned thanks: the band then played the National Anthem, and the waiters cleared the tables. The streets were now crowded, and the numbers are variously estimated; from 25,000 to 30,000 persons were assembled, anxiously waiting for the other interesting fetes of the day. *(This seems a slight exaggeration!)*.

And their patience was not long tried; for very soon, the children of the church and Wesleyan Sunday Schools arrived, headed by their pastors and superintendents, and the *Bedfordshire Militia Band*; these were joined by the Baptist schools, headed by the *Dunstable and London Band*, marching from the Free school down to the Post Office, up the Albion Road to the Tabernacle, where they received another addition from the schools of that place, and proceeding onward they came to the Primitive-Methodist chapel, and were

---

*The word 'bonfire' has also been said to be derived from 'bone fire', where the bones of deceased persons of earlier periods were burnt to make room for further burials.

joined by the school, headed by the celebrated *Morfey Band*.

After marching round the town, the children of the various schools to the number of 1,200, sat down to tea on the Square, where an unlimited supply of cake and tea was provided for them.

After the children had done ample justice to the repast provided, all adjourned to a meadow, where the *Militia and Morfey Bands* amused the company, and all kinds of innocent amusements were carried on. Another company, headed by the *London Band*, proceeded to a meadow near the ancient recreation ground, known as the Butts, and there spent the evening until the time arrived for the thousands to disperse to witness the illuminations and fireworks.

Most of the principal manufacturers and tradesmen illuminated their houses, and amongst the most tasteful were the decorations at the different solicitors' offices, and a triumphal arch across the road, with Chinese lamps at the Sugar Loaf, and a handsome gas star joining the Market House. At ten o'clock in the evening, a splendid display of fireworks commenced which gave great satisfaction.

A few of the manufacturers gave their sewers* a private entertainment the same day, and the factory yards exhibited a pleasing spectacle, being tastefully decorated with foliage and flowers; while Messrs. Munt and Brown reserved their treat for the following day, which consisted of a good tea and supper, with bands of music to play during the refreshment, so we are of opinion that all parties have been well cared for.

Per W. H. Derbyshire with extracts from the Dunstaplelogia – written by Mr Charles Lamborn, formerly headmaster of the British School, and lecturer in Natural Philosophy, published by James Tibbett in 1859.

The tinted picture opposite, taken in the late 1800s, shows Messrs. Munt & Brown's hat factory in High St. South next to Priory House, on the right of the picture. The building was later demolished to allow for access to the then newly developing Priory Gardens, and adjacent redevelopments in the right foreground. The left mid section of the photo shows the area of the 'Square' with the end buildings to Middle Row still recognisable. The two figures on the bottom left are approaching the present day site of the 'Millennium Clock'.

To the left of the Square (mid left) can be seen part of the old buildings behind Middle Row long since demolished, where in 2003 the access to Wilkinsons and the other shops lining the east side of Ashton Street are to be found. The Square has for a long time past been the site of various civic etc. celebrations, with the buildings on each flank showing as backdrops to many historic photographs. The era of the photo can be underlined by the single horse and cart proceeding casually along the middle of the High Street.(See also 24. June 1856 report on earlier page).

---

* This term refers to the employees who sew the material.(Ed.)

MESSRS. MUNT & BROWN'S HAT FACTORY IN HIGH STREET SOUTH

The origin of the photo is not identified other than 'printed in Saxony'. – AW

Dunstable Chronicle

12 Jan 1856
Adverts

Miss Dinah Donne, daughter of E. B. Donne, Professor of Music, will receive a selected number of pupils at separate ages and prices. Includes Music & Singing etc at 10/6d per quarter. Also Advert: Tibbetts 'Musical Bouquet' sheets at 3d.

General Editorial

Referred to Dunstable's low status and treatment with respect to police, lock-up etc.

Letter

From Edward Burr stating his thanks to the leading citizens of the town on his leaving Dunstable.

5 April 1856
Editorial

Re peace celebrations, referring to the town's decorations and the Priory bells.

Letter

Recalling the allies entering Paris in 1814!

19 April 1856
Advert

The Morfey family – including six children – (well known entertainers over a wide area), performed a programme of vocal and instrumental music at a concert in the Temperance Hall.

Letter

Championing the femininity of local women (bonnet sewers) in a reference to annual hiring days in Aylesbury.

21 June 1856
Editorial

Peace festival, programme of events, and a reference to the British Girls' School, with a comment recalling the 'Dame' schools of 30 years ago.

27 June 1856
Report Peace Festival – referred to the celebrated 'Dunstable Brass Band', the bells of the Priory Church, the band of the Bed's Militia, a London Band, Free School boys, the Morfey Band, and on Wednesday, the Hemel Hempstead Choir.

5 July 1856
Report Dunstable – Fire Brigade Fete & Holiday – A very long report describes the Brigades attending from a wide area, with the flags, banners, decorations etc and the presence of several bands including: The St. Albans Juvenile Band, The Thame Band, Other [un-named] bands.

A concert was performed, including several London professionals who had also been engaged for the occasion. Afterwards, there was cricket, trap & ball, cock-shie, kiss-in-the-ring, Punch and Judy. 3000–4000 were said to be present.

21 Nov 1856
Report Dunstable Choral Society – at the Temperance Hall with 'King Pippin Polka', 'Sultan', and 'Fairy Polka', performed by a newly raised band composed of young men of the town. Solo vocals, the Glees. Others sang 'The Soldier's Tear', and 'Mary of Argyll'. (Also a Temperance Society report).

19 Dec 1856
Report The Dunstable Choral and Instrumental Society held its second concert at the Temperance Hall in aid of a new and modern Fire Engine. £5 was raised but there was a caution against spending the proceeds on eating, drinking and smoking!

This was followed by a report on the concert similar to previous occasions, though simply highlighting the performance of the 'Mary Ann Quadrille' by name.

Advert 'Household Almanac,' which included the 'Value of a good wife'; 'Good and bad temper'; and rather extraordinarily – '12 ways to commit suicide'!

3 Feb 1856 to
27 Sept 1856
Obituary Mr. Braham, the noted musician [from London] who often stayed at the 'Sugar Loaf' Hotel.

Reports Professor E.B. Donne performed at the piano in the Temperance Hall.
[A pistol shooting contest was to take place at the 'Saracen's Head'.]
The Leighton Buzzard Oddfellows engaged a band from London who performed 'The Fall of Sebastopol' and the National Anthem.
The Toddington Brass Band played at their Peace celebrations with the Morfey Family from London.
90 members of the Oddfellows sat down at the 'Saracen's Head' for dinner. The Dunstable Brass Band played 'Rule Britannia', and songs were performed by the Chairman and others to the accompaniment of the Band.
The Association of Tradesmen Friendly Society met – and the Brass Band played.
The Houghton Regis rural festival was held in July – the [village's] Brass Band played.
A new organ was installed in the Baptist Church, similar to many in the area by the same builder.

10 Jan 1857

Editorial　　This took the form of a moral article about Christmas.

Report　　The Dunstable Choral and Instrumental Society held its third 'People's Concert' at the Temperance Hall. Fewer attended on this occasion. It was reported that 'The small but effective band played admirably . . . the 'Windsor Quadrilles' . . . especially pleasing . . . Soloists also sang . . .'

Report　　Toddington – A tea meeting and concert of sacred music was held . . . 80 persons attended. There were selections from the 'Messiah' and other works. A vote of thanks was made to the 'Ladies and Gentlemen of the Orchestra' . . . proceeds were to go to side galleries in the Wesleyan chapel.

5 June 1857
Report　　Totternhoe – Members of the 'Cross Keys' Benefit Society held their annual feast, when the 'Brass Band from Eaton Bray' was in attendance. After dining, and drinking the landlord's home brewed ale, they marched through the village playing some of their tunes to farmers at their homes, receiving a can of good ale each time!

The senior members headed the band, while the younger members followed, giving an entertainment by a few good dances and some homely rural songs. As the band was about to leave they were asked to favour members with the National Anthem, to which the leader at once complied, but through taking the wrong key, struck up the 'Old Hundred' tune – he was stopped by the others, and tried again, but struck up 'Rule Britannia' which was performed in good style! He then tried again with better success and gave the National Anthem to the satisfaction of all parties.'

(This is so far the only known reference to the Eaton Bray Brass Band – Ed.).

27 June 1857
Reports　　Sewell – A rural treat: – Teachers and pupils of West Street Baptist schools went to Manor Farm by invitation of Mr. George Scroggs for tea etc, at his farmhouse which had been leased since 1759.

A new safety carriage to take 70 persons was constructed by Bowden & Cheshire. Mr. Gutteridge lent two horses and Mr. Scroggs his large wagon and horses.

300 were there for tea in the orchard . . . Cricket, racing and football were played. There was singing in the evening by 200 voices. Later the children returned with buns by the 'Safety' wagon etc. Villagers were amazed by the numbers there. It was a great and unusual treat for many.

Berkhamsted – An Oddfellows Gala was held, attended by the 'Life Guards Band' and people from a wide area. There was a 'Quadrille' band, games etc; [some drunken behaviour amazed residents]. Special trains were arranged by the LNW Line.

24 July 1857
Article　　Dunstable, Grand Annual Children's Holiday – Thursday last – in the Park. The Band of the Beds. Militia was lent by Adjutant Toseland, arriving from Bedford early a.m. – it marched up the town headed by the committee and friends, flags, banners etc.. The LNWR train from Leighton Buzzard, and other conveyances from Luton, Markyate Street and other places, were in place by 2.00 o'clock.

Children from Sunday schools met at the Park and proceeded up and down the High St., Church St., West St., Albion St., Edward St., Mount St. and Union St. to the Park. 800 children were seated (girls on the right, boys on the left), with a Band in the middle.

Football, cricket, quoits and other games were played. Tea was served at 4.00pm. The children romped and rolled merrily . . . until evening. The Band accompanied the old 100th psalm and the national anthem. T. Cheshire, G. Stevenson, and professor E. B. Donne, taught the children to sing. Speeches were then made on the necessity of recreation . . . several other persons were present – 2178 entered by ticket (which) with 800 children numbered 3000, sale of tickets raised £27.5.0d.'

15 Aug 1857
Report

Cricket Match – at Luton. E. Vyse's 22 versus a United England 11 who won. 2 innings were played and the England team included a Mr Wisden! 3000 watched.

26 June 1858
Advert

For the Dunstable Fire Brigade Grand Fete and Holiday on the 9th July 1858. The brigade will drive and process with engines, Bands of music, banners and flags etc., to a dinner in the Park. Grace to be sung by pros! Bands will play favourite pieces through dinner. This to be followed by sports and pastimes in 'Four Corners' with Mr Fraser and his 'Crystal Palace'. A Grand concert with London artists in the evening. Balloons, a public tea at 9d. each. Special trains . . . triumphal arches . . . Admission 1s. (9d. under 12).

Report

The Rev. Hose, Rector. A report of a party held at Mr. Medland's – tributes were paid to the Rev. Hose, with thanks for his improved health. He replied, and promised increased exertions on their behalf according to his strength etc.

Advert

Ginnett's Circus with feats of horsemanship (no mention of a Band).

Report

A grand musical entertainment at the Temperance Hall, featuring the 'tonic sol-fa' System of musical notation.

1 Nov 1858
Reports

Mechanics institute, Edward street. The opening took place – with H. Brandreth, Osborn, Farr, Elliot, Lockhart. 100 members already.

Objects – for the religious, moral, scientific and practical improvements of the young men of the town. (Fuller report the following week). The Institute was founded in Manchester in 1836 for the improvement in the education and moral improvement of young men.

Toddington, Wesleyan day school – 'the Englishman'.

The Harmonic Society
'Lovers of music, excelling . . . Attending first public meeting – similar throughout the country.'
(Music as a science is no longer confined to the cloister or palace . . .')

(*N.B. Douglas Darby recalls that the hall referred to above in Edward Street where the Mechanics Institute was reported to have met was not built until*

1864, and that the 'Chronicle' report may have mistaken the venue, it possibly being the old Temperance Hall at the corner of West Street and Victoria Street – a building that was afterwards demolished and was the precursor of Moreton House School – itself long since demolished, and these days the site of Carlton House. – Ed)

Editorial   Parliamentary reform discussed – (Mr. Gladstone, Chancellor).

16 June 1859
Report   Toddington – Oddfellows annual festival at The 'Sow and Pigs'. A large procession, with personnel in full regalia, was headed by *The Toddington Brass Band*. The report mentions speeches, toasts, and vocal and instrumental renditions, all ending in good order.

20 June 1859
Article   Fire Brigade Fete and Holiday: Report on the event describing decorations, flags, arches, the priory – flag and bells, The Band of the Grenadier Guards. Seven arches welcoming fire brigades from a wide area, Leighton Buzzard, Dunstable, Hemel Hempstead, Berkhamstead, St Albans, Newport Pagnell and Markyate. The boys of the 'endowed school' (Chew's School) followed a large procession of brigades and bands. The day was spoiled by rain. Dinner was served in a tent with the Grenadier Guards Band playing. Other acts and entertainments took part. Sports were played, and speeches and toasts, with 4,000 to 5,000 present in the evening. (See programme of the procession).

The programme for the procession lists the various Fire Brigades, describing each Engine, and mounted personnel: the uniforms and decorations, and the name of each superintendent. Four bands were placed within the procession, headed by The Band of the Grenadier Guards.

Article   A correspondent from Woburn describes a 'Day at Dunstable', (not mentioning the above festival), recalling a cricket match 35 years earlier in 'Crow Field' – which by now was 'settled down in streets, houses and gardens'! The writer describes the Priory and its history, and also mentions Woburn, Toddington, Ridgmont and Bedford, and refers to historic associations that celebrate Bedfordshire's role – a distinction not always recorded and appreciated! The approach by Chalk Hill was 'a world esteemed locality', the plait buyers leaving in the early morning, with crowds flocking to 'the Bazaar' opened with an address by Lord Russell in aid of the Wesleyan Funds.
(This was the reason for the visit it would seem – Ed.)

Music c. BC 200 – W. G. Smith's Lecture 1889

In 1889, the celebrated historian – and the first Freeman of the Borough of Dunstable, Mr. Worthington George Smith (pictured) – gave a lecture in Dunstable entitled 'The Music and Musical Instruments of the Barbarians'. This derived from his own research into early man and material supplied from the Reverend G. W. Torrence's then recent visit to Australia, and the Aboriginal people.

W. G. Smith was an internationally renowned expert on fungi, and a noted expert in the developing subject of Archaeology. He had written a book called 'Man, The Primeval Savage', and was a celebrated pioneer in the subject. He regularly lectured on early man, but this particular event was somewhat unique.

'THE MUSIC AND MUSICAL INSTRUMENTS OF THE BARBARIANS' – 1889

'Smith had made his own version of primitive instruments which he endeavoured to play. He then called upon Miss Marie Tatagni, and his younger son Edward (Smith): To play three airs taken down by the Reverend G. W. Torrence, from the actual performance of the original inhabitants of Australia.'*

" As you listen to these three genuine airs of barbarians you may reasonably imagine yourself on Dunstable Downs, two thousand years ago, listening to a prehistoric concert. I must leave you to imagine an accompaniment of drum, rattle, squealer, horn, whistle and bones, with the never absent hand-clapping and foot-stamping ". (WGS)

* This performance was on piano and violin!

The lecture was featured in BHRS. Vol 57, 1978, 'W. G. Smith & other studies'.

BRASS BANDS

3 THE RIFLE VOLUNTEERS BAND

The Rifle Volunteers and their Band

As mentioned in an earlier chapter the (Rifle) Volunteers were local units originally founded to augment the Regular Militia at the time of the first Napoleonic wars c.1795–1805, and for a period following. The town of Dunstable provided a company as part of the (South) Bedfordshire Rifle Volunteers.

After the danger of a Napoleonic invasion was past with victory over the French, the Volunteers were eventually disbanded. However later in the 19th century the danger returned when a 'New Napoleon' tried to blockade Britain and posed a renewed threat to the country, and the threat of invasion arose again.

The date was 1859 when it was proposed to re-instate the Volunteers over the whole of the country, in a somewhat similar role to today's Territorial Army. In fact later on, in 1908, the Volunteers were merged with the newly instituted Territorials and were thereby disbanded as a separate force.

The military had a tradition of bands of musicians to support the troops and sometimes lead into battle. This is dealt with in the chapter on the development of the Brass Band movement. When the Volunteers were re-formed in 1859, a few of the veterans of the earlier brigades were still around and joined again.

The Town already appears to have had a Brass Band c.1855 or earlier. The evidence of this is to be found in reports in Dunstable's first newspaper the 'Dunstable Chronicle', referring to local events and which featured the 'Town's Brass Band' on several occasions, but in which there is no mention of a date of foundation or the names of any of the musicians. However, on the re-formation of the Volunteers there appeared to be enough musical resources in the town for the company to form its own Band. The Franklin family was to the fore in this respect as we shall see from another chapter.

The Volunteer Band was to become a sort of parallel organisation to the newly-formed Borough Band, with the Franklin family supplying – over a period of time – ten playing members involved with both bands.

The Volunteers' Uniform

According to Joyce Godber's 'History of Bedfordshire', the South Beds. Volunteers' uniform was grey with green decoration, and included the familiar 'Shako' hat, similar to the hats worn later on by the Confederate Army in the American Civil War c.1865. The shakos would be decorated with a cockade of white feathers added for special occasions. (The North Beds. (Horse) volunteers were rather more resplendent however in red tunics and white trousers!)

Below is a picture of a Volunteer taken in 1875, actually from the Lewes, Sussex company but sent to an ancestor of the author, showing a cup won in a drill competition by the company commanded by the gentleman in the photo. We can see the typical uniform as described by Joyce Godber. The condition of the photo tends to obscure the height of the shako which is taller than the dark band alone.

Some 'Yesteryear' photographs in the 'Gazette' of the early thirties showed bands of 30 to 50 years earlier in a military style uniform and wearing shakos – typical headwear – sporting ceremonial feathers.

The Volunteers' Review of 1877

One fascinating event that took place locally, was the Volunteers' Review held in Dunstable & district on the Easter Monday, 1877, some eighteen years after their refounding, with units from a wide area of the south of England & London meeting for a series of mock battles on the outskirts of the town.

A large procession with several bands paraded through the town, including of course the local company, with the salute being taken in High St. North. There are no photographs of the event, but a Dunstable resident, Mr. F.A.Cassidy of Burr Street, had some engravings of the occasion and two of these are reproduced in the following pages. (Sadly Mr. Cassidy, a relative of the Dolman family, has recently died.)

The following pages show details of the 1877 Review including information from the Gazette of 4th April 1877, and from two engravings of the event drawn from the processions parading through the centre of Dunstable – two somewhat unique records of the occasion also contributed by Mr. Cassidy to the Gazette's 'Bygones' series in the 6th October 1993 edition.

THE VOLUNTEERS' REVIEW OF 1877

This illustration shows part of an engraving of the Volunteers' Review on Easter Monday 1877, when Volunteer Brigades and their Bands came to Dunstable from all over the Southern area of England including London to take part in a series of mock battles staged over an area from Dunstable Downs and Totternhoe Knolls, to Stanbridge Ford, Maiden Bower and Eaton Bray. The engraving shows part of the procession through Dunstable with certain features of High Street North, as seen from the crossroads, still recognisable over 100 years later. The picture shows the Volunteers headed by a Brass or Military Band as the marchers pass the officer reviewing seated on horseback roughly outside the place where 'The Woolwich' is in the year 2000.

N.B. In a guide to Dunstable for the year 1900, there is a rare entry for the Volunteers:
'*Volunteer Battalion (3rd) Bedfordshire Regiment (D Co. Capt. L. Newton: Serg't Major James Sheppard, drill instructor), Head-quarters, 92, West Street.*'

Troops had arrived in Dunstable from London and elsewhere by road and special trains, and included the London Scottish Brigade led by a piper playing 'Bonnie Dundee'. The event was described in great detail in the Gazette of Wednesday 4th April 1877. The Gazette's report stated that between 10,000 and 11,000 troops took part and an estimated 30,000 spectators watched the 'battles' from the Downs & other vantage points as they took place during the

THE VOLUNTEERS' REVIEW OF 1877, FURTHER DETAIL

The wider picture shown on the earlier page has been divided into two parts and enlarged as shown below.

The Band can be more clearly seen in the lower picture.

(FC/DG)

morning of the 2nd of April 1877 until approx 2.00 p.m. This must have been a spectacular event in its own right and for the people of Dunstable and district in particular, and it is something of a revelation that such an event should have been staged in and around Dunstable, although the estimates of the numbers of those present could perhaps have been a little optimistic!

1877 RIFLE VOLUNTEERS' REVIEW 'WELCOME' ARCH WEST STREET

This is taken from another engraving supplied to the 'Gazette' by Mr. Cassidy in 1993 for their 'Bygones' series. The engraving depicts one of four ceremonial arches in the town. The viewpoint of the picture is from a position facing the North-West junction of West Street and High Street North. The buildings are still recognisable although changed over the years.

Below: A Photo from the 'Gazette' of 17th December 1930. The caption says, that the 'origin of the picture is obscure', that it was taken '50 years ago' (which would date it at 1880), and that 'it cannot be the Volunteers – as they did not wear cockades'! (but see earlier page reference to Joyce Godber's History of Bedfordshire which states that the Volunteers wore cockades for special occasions).

POSSIBLY THE OLDEST PICTURE OF A DUNSTABLE BRASS BAND

It can be seen that there are twelve men sporting feather cockades with one without, also there is a 'civilian' on the left wearing a straw hat and formal dress. There are two players with a drum each: a bass drum – centre, and a side drum to the left. These would indicate an essentially marching Band. The military style uniforms and headgear, together with the two drums, point to this being the 4th-Beds. Rifle Volunteers Band, c.1880.

The Volunteers were to continue until 1908, when, as mentioned earlier, they were disbanded and merged with the Territorials. This was seen to be an appropriate move in the military developments of the twentieth century.

As far as the Band and its musicians were concerned, the Old Borough Band was to continue for another thirty years, with the Franklin family still carrying on their volunteer traditions in that brass band, as featured in the following chapter.

4 THE DUNSTABLE BOROUGH BRASS BAND

The earliest known photo of the Band (below), was taken in early 1905 at the rear of the 'Horse & Jockey' public house on the A5, Watling Street, Kensworth.

THE DUNSTABLE BOROUGH BRASS BAND 1905

(JS)

The band at the 'Horse & Jockey' public house in Kensworth 1905. The group includes: (l – r) 'Moke', with the bass drum; William Bull, a guest on this occasion from the Excelsior Band (Jim Bull's father); Perce More; George Franklin; Septimus Franklin; and Edward Franklin; together with one or two others to be identified.

The photo was supplied by a grand-daughter of Edward Franklin, Mrs. Jane Stanley now living in Eversholt. Edward was one of ten of his family who played for the Borough Band and also the Rifle Volunteers. Edward became one of the great personalities of the Town and the Band.

The origins and development of this Band are well described in an informative and now rather rare booklet produced in1907 by a Mr. Williams of Luton, who reviewed Brass Bands in Luton & District, but did not include the Leighton Buzzard area. An edited extract about the Band is set out on the following pages.

The Dunstable Borough Brass Band was also known as Franklin's Band or the 'Beer & Baccy' Band

Extract from the 1907 Booklet

'This band was first formed as a (Rifle)Volunteer Band about the year 1860. The first bandmaster was Mr. Henry Farrer, who was succeeded by Mr W. Walters. On the retirement of this gentleman, the late Mr. Henry Watson held the position for some time. He was followed by the late Mr. George Franklin, who was bandmaster for 35 years, having been a playing member from the band's first formation – a period of 45 years. The present bandmaster is Mr Frederick Franklin.

'The playing of the band, in its early history, was thought a lot of, and so much satisfaction did they give wherever they were engaged that some of the engagements have been booked for a number of years in succession.At the Long Marston Benefit Societies' annual club feast they have attended 35 years in succession; Leighton Buzzard Friendly Societies' anniversaries 36 years; and Milton Bryant Garden Party 35 years.

'At Lord Brownlow's local seat, Ashridge Park, they attended the Harvest Festivals for twenty years. They have also visited London, Peterborough, Oundle, Brackley, Kidlington and other places. When the Brewer's Hill right-of-way case was being fought on behalf of the public, and was ultimately won, this band took a prominent part. The band is occasionally referred to as 'Franklin's band', for several brothers and their sons of this well-known Dunstable family were in the band.

"When the public read the career of these musical brothers as brass bandsmen, I think they will agree with me that their record is one that would be hard to equal, and I doubt if it could be excelled in the whole of England.

'The following is the record of the 'Franklin Musical Family' and their years of service in this one band as at 1907:

The late Mr. George Franklin	45 years
Mr. James Franklin	45 years
Mr. Edward Franklin	43 years
Mr. Septimus Franklin	42 years
Mr. Henry Franklin	34 years
Mr. Frederick Franklin	34 years

An advert from the booklet.

'When Mr. George Franklin was the bandmaster he was assisted by his five brothers, with his only son William, and brothers' sons to the number of three, making a total number of 10 members of the band of the name of Franklin. At the time the booklet was produced (1907) Mr. Henry Franklin was also bandmaster of the Fenny Stratford Prize Band.

'There were then living ten members of the family of Franklin who were all efficient brass band performers. Six brothers aggregated about 200 years service as brass band instrumentalists and four brothers' sons over 60 years, together a period of 260 years. Mr Frederick James Franklin, son of James Franklin, and the oldest son of the brothers Franklin had been a member of the band for 32 years.

'Five of the Franklin family were holders of the long service medal in connection with the Volunteers. I think truly, the Franklins have a marvellous record. There is every appearance that it will be many years before the name of Franklin will be eliminated from brass bands in the royal borough of Dunstable.

'Mr Septimus Franklin has at one time or another played every instrument – drums included. The band still have rehearsals under Mr. Fred Franklin, and are always willing and capable of meeting any engagement that comes along, great or small.

'There are several other bandsmen in this band who are not Franklins, and when they all meet for rehearsals they constitute a fairly good band. Some few years back they attended a band contest at Luton, and were awarded the second prize. The band had been specially rehearsed for this contest by the well-known band trainer Mr. J. T. Ogden. If they are not so strong in numbers, and their playing is not quite up to some of the contesting bands of the district, the Dunstable Borough Band always give satisfaction wherever they are engaged. *Per 1907 Booklet – Williams. (fin)*

As we have seen, the Borough Band developed from the band formed from the local Rifle Volunteers, re-instituted in 1859. The core of both bands seems to have been the Franklin family of Dunstable, whose members of various generations volunteered their services to the 4th Bedfordshire Rifle Volunteers, and formed a large part of the Volunteer Band. They then combined with others to form the Borough Brass Band from c1864, the year in which Dunstable obtained its (second) Charter as a Borough.

The band also earned its nickname, the 'Beer and Baccy' band from its base at the 'White Horse' public house in Church Street, and from its tradition of playing through the town, calling at various inns and hostelries, the musicians refreshing themselves in the process and pausing for a smoke of tobacco. Opposite the 'White Horse' was one of several drill halls in Dunstable. This later became Rixon's Antiques, and today is the premises of the 'Book Castle'.

If the Excelsior Band was founded as a Temperance band, then the Borough Band can surely be considered as "fully licensed"!

THE WHITE HORSE, CHURCH STREET

Two Views of 'The White Horse' Church Street in the early 20th Century. The pub was the Headquarters of the Borough Band, with Septimus Franklin 'mine Host'

This photograph was taken in the early years of the 20th century and is one of two or three taken at the same time, each with minor differences. This is a much larger gathering than the opening picture and shows the Band with supporters aboard the Band's own specially built Wagonette. There appears to be about a dozen men with instruments – none of whom are 'on stage' though!

THE BOROUGH BAND 'ON THE ROAD'

(MD)

This horse-drawn vehicle served both as transport and as a stage for the Band's various forays into the surrounding towns and villages. It is not known at present where this photo was taken however. The 'Wagonette' must have been of sturdy build, to support the large number of people on board.

This photograph shows the Borough Band (Franklin's Band), playing in High Street South Dunstable, probably on a Saturday afternoon outside Messrs. Moore's shop & the adjoining premises sometime in the early 20th century.

OUTSIDE MOORE'S SHOP

The photograph clearly shows the identity of the whole range of premises covered by the scene, The 'Bun House', and 'Paris House' in particular being named. The 'International Stores' is the shop to the left of these premises. Moore's premises are to the right of the picture.
(Photograph – Courtesy Mrs. P. Keen)

The Franklin Family of Dunstable

The story really starts with John Franklin(1st), born in Leighton Buzzard c1785, who moved to Dunstable where he became the publican at the White Horse, Church Street, and surprisingly combined this role with the post of Town Constable. He married Sophie Parkins in 1804, and they had three sons, the youngest of whom also called John (2nd) was born in 1820. The accounts of John (lst's) experiences as Town Constable make interesting reading on their own, but are somewhat outside the scope of this project. John (2nd) married Elizabeth Crouch and took over the 'White Horse' from his father, in due course. He was also described as a straw bonnet blocker. He and Elizabeth had ten children – nine sons and one daughter. (There is no record of him playing an instrument). Sophie, the last of the ten, was born in 1860. She was later recorded as running the 'Sugar Loaf Tap'.

The second son John (3rd) died in 1863 in Nottingham, aged 23 years. The 5th son Charles (born 1847), also died in Nottingham (age not known). Neither of these two is recorded as playing in a band. The other six as below all played: also four members of the next generation are recorded as musicians.

Name	Born	(Died)	(Volunteers) started 1859 Age	(Boro' Band) Double Charter Age in 1864	Age in 1907
(4) George	1838	1904 (66)	21	26	(dec'd)
(1) James	1842	1909 (67)	17	22	65
(2) Edward	1849	1918 (69)	10	15	58
(3) Septimus	1851	1932 (81)	8	13	56
Fred'ck	1858	* *	*	6	49
(5) # *	*	* *	*	*	*
(6) Henry (dates o/s)		* *	*	*	*

(1) Son James Frederick also played in the band.

(2) Edward married Jane Cook of Eversholt, in 1871. Their son, Edgar, married Susan Adams, and their daughter, Jane Stanley, has been the source of so much of this information. Edward took over the 'White Horse' from his father.

(3) Septimus took over after Edward died in 1918. Septimus, as his name suggests, was the seventh child of John (2nd), and was still playing in 1924 at the age of 73.

(4) Another son, William, (son of George) also played, with two others.

(5) Two other sons – not named.(#)

(6) Henry was also Bandmaster with the Fenny Stratford Prize Band.

Edward Franklin – Newspaper Reports

Edward, pictured overleaf as a scholar at Chew's school, was to become celebrated for his service to the town, and for his exploits, particularly in the 'Battle of Brewers Hill' in 1891, the removal of the tollgate (south of the town on the Watling Street) c1900, and the Church Street Enclosures. He was elected Mayor in 1911, 1916 & 1917.

The Dunstable Borough Gazette – 7.11.1894 Here the main story relates to the enclosures and encroachments in Church Street, in particular the dispute over the frontage of Kingsbury House where the land (after various ownership claims) had been fenced off with posts and chains. The Gazette heralded the appearance of Edward Franklin, the champion of Brewers Hill who made a speech to the Council and townspeople, stating his analysis of ownership and claiming the land as public land.

He led a meeting at the site, and, after a declaration of legal rights, proceeded to remove the posts and chains (continuing the following day). Once

EDWARD AS A SCHOOLBOY

(JS/
AV

The photograph shows Edward Franklin as a scholar at 'The Endowed School' as Chew's School was often referred to, wearing the uniform of the day c.1860. Each pupil was given a leather bound copy of the Bible, Edward's being in the possession of Mrs. Jane Stanley and containing family details in the traditional manner.

again the Borough Band was present, and among other things gave a lively rendition of 'For he's a jolly good fellow'.

The next report in the same issue, related to the ensuing council elections, in which Edward Franklin was placed at the bottom of the poll! – a sorry reward for his efforts for the town. Edward Franklin made a humorous speech however, thanking the voters for their efforts in keeping him off the council this time.

Here the report describes the attendance and musical contributions of the Excelsior band who played well received selections while the results were being counted – no mention of the Borough Band on this occasion though!

The Gazette 15th November 1911 In this report, Edward is quoted as saying 'his memory went back to the time he marched in the Volunteer Band at the proclamation of the Town's Charter in 1864, six months after leaving Chew's school' and referred to his record of service to the Town since that occasion. (He didn't mention the instrument he played however).

The same issue also reported the Mayoral Service, and a dinner at Marchant's restaurant (a Temperance establishment).

The report quotes 'The Borough Band under Mr. F. Franklin ably played a choice selection of music'. The procession to the Priory Church had included the Mace Bearer, Mr. Coombes, now attired in uniform . . . the Church Lads' Brigade, the local Territorial Corps under Sergeant Odell, and council members (the fire brigade acting as a guard of honour).

As the procession entered the Church, and on the return journey, the band played appropriate selections (the procession later returned to the Town Hall).

The Borough Band in 1911 would still have included Septimus and Henry, with Frederick conducting. Edward of course, as Mayor, would presumably not have joined in on this occasion! The four sons were probably present, although they are not referred to – neither were Septimus or Henry – but it would be surprising if at the ages of 61 & 59 they were not there.

No mention is made of members of the Volunteers being present on this occasion, as they had of course been superseded by the Territorials.

Another early picture of the Borough Band, probably about 1910.

'The Battle of Brewers Hill'

The following page shows two of a set of cartoons published in 1891 to celebrate the winning of the High Court case by Edward Franklin & Co. to keep the Brewers Hill pathway a public right of way, beating the L.& N.W. Railway Co. & Mr. Cook the farmer – the result was heralded by the Borough Band who were present at all stages.

Brewers Hill Road at that time was a country lane, leading from the Watling Street, north of Dunstable (then in Upper Houghton Regis), past Cook's farm, and at a point near to Green Lanes turned left – becoming what is now Drovers Way, and ending at its junction with West Street.

The L.&N.W.Railway Co. had built the line to Leighton Buzzard in 1846 and older Dunstablians will remember the level crossing gates in Brewers Hill that were opened and closed by the gatekeeper. (The old turntable site is commemorated in the grounds of the South Beds. DC offices in High Street North, in a design that follows its original shape).

The lane was used by farmer Cook & the locals generally in a somewhat sporadic way and all was peaceable until 1888 when an Enclosure Commission report for Totternhoe defined the lane as a Highway. This upset both farmer Cook & the Railway Co.who did not want an increase in all and sundry now wanting to pass over the crossing. The latter parties decided to lock the gates against the public, and claimed the road as a private road. This led to an ongoing controversy which festered until January 1890, when as a result of certain meetings in Houghton Regis it was decided that something should be done to reclaim the highway.

Edward Franklin who was a public spirited Dunstablian thought that he and his townspeople should take the initiative in this matter and rallied a large crowd (with the help of the Town Crier – a post still in existence then) and persuaded Mr. Cook to open the gates.

Edward became a local Councillor from 1898 to 1918 (& Mayor 1911–1912, & 1916–1918). He was a carpenter by trade and one of a large family (qv), and as we know a member of the Borough Brass Band. He arranged for the band to head the procession (said to have been 5000 in number), eight of the band being Franklins.

The notice board erected by the farmer & the railway was torn down and destroyed.

However the gates were later locked again and this pattern continued until a High Court action in London by Edward and his associates was successful.The success was celebrated by an exciting homecoming by Edward who was met at the Church St. station by large crowds and of course – the Band, who played 'For He's a Jolly Good Fellow' and 'See The Conquering Hero Come', amongst others.

An article in the Dunstable & District Local History Society newsletter (no.6) relates that a fortnight later a crowd of nearly 10,000 plus several Bands paraded up and down Brewers Hill & Drovers Way, following a public notice advertising the event, which took place on December 10th 1891, starting from the Town Hall at 2.00 p.m. The notice asked that 'no unseemly demonstration of any kind take place while passing Mr. Cook's farm'. 'Tea was to be provided at the Town Hall at 4.30 p.m. by the Committee for subscribers and witnesses'.

It was reported that good order was maintained.

EDWARD FRANKLIN AND 'THE BATTLE OF BREWERS HILL' 1891

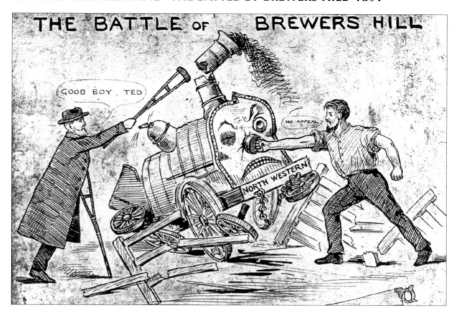

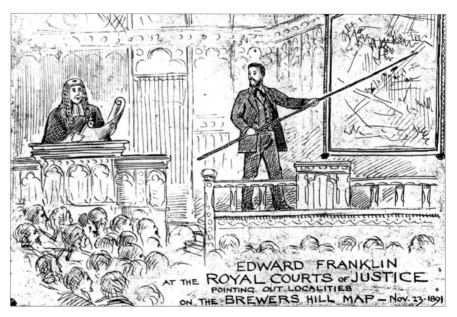

The Cartoons – Courtesy of Mrs. Jane Stanley, Edward's great grand-daughter.

Thus the Borough Brass Band (advertised as The Dunstable Brass Band), the Franklins, and Edward in particular played a notable part in this important event, saving Brewers Hill as a public highway.

The record of the Court proceedings are far too long for inclusion here, but make interesting and amusing reading, including reports of several older and sometimes rustic witnesses recounting their courting days in the Brewers Hill lane as it was then.

PAMPHLET 10TH DECEMBER 1891

WHO IS FRANKLIN?

As the Public Right-of-way dispute, now styled "The Battle of Brewers Hill," will no doubt be circulated far and wide, many will naturally ask the question, "Who is Franklin?" The brief answer will be, that he is of humble parentage, and a journeyman carpenter; that he is 42 years of age, has a wife and four children, and lives in a cottage, 99, Church Street, Dunstable, which habitation is the very type of home comforts and cleanliness.

Edward Franklin is one of a family of nine boys and a girl. Strange to say, the boys were all born musicians, six of them being now in the Dunstable Borough Band and the Volunteer Band, and eight of the nine (now men grown) are church and hand-bell ringers. Edward was educated at the Free School, Dunstable, and as a boy did credit to that noble charity by his attention to the privileges afforded him. As a boy he was generous, open-hearted, and always had the courage of his opinion : hence the man whom we delight to honour on this 10th day of December, 1891, at the celebration of the re-opening of Brewers Hill public right-of-way. Too much praise cannot be accorded to him for his indomitable courage, tact, and wisdom in this great undertaking. Great credit is due to him also in the wise selection of his committee, viz., two from each of the following places—Luton, Dunstable, Toddington, and Houghton Regis. Each person was selected for his known ability for such important work. Good judgment was shewn in their selection of Mr. Councillor Thomas Cox, of Cheapside, Luton, as their chairman, who, to show his interest in the case, never omitted to attend a single meeting. The fact, probably, is known but to few, that at one time a very heavy demand for money was made in order that the case could be brought to trial. Be it known that Mr. Cox (Chairman), Mr. Batchelor, brewer, of Dagnall, and Mr. Evans, of Chalk Hill, Dunstable, came to the rescue, and the trial proceeded and ended with the happy result of a victory for Franklin. Much credit is due to him in his selection of witnesses, numbering some forty or more. Franklin, therefore, has merited a people's gratitude for the victory gained, and the noble example he has set as a conservator of the Rights of the People.

T. C. JOHNSON, Senr.

(JS)

The pamphlet gives details of Edward Franklin and 'Brewers Hill'.

PEACE CELEBRATIONS 19TH JULY 1919 – THE BOROUGH BAND IN PROCESSION

After the Great War

The above is an enlarged section of a photo taken from the Peace Celebration Souvenir Programme. A band can just be identified following the young people at the front of the picture. This appears most likely to be the Borough Band (Franklin's Band) as it appears to be in a different section of the procession to that which includes the Excelsior Silver Prize Band.

In mid picture can be seen the cattle market pens, though it is not clear as to the figures situated within the area. It could perhaps be a space for small children, or just the general public. The buildings in the background have largely been replaced or refurbished but the view will be familiar to older Dunstablians, and the general aspect may still be recognisable in spite of the changes that have taken place. This part of the procession is approaching the Square along High Street South, near to the current position of the new Millennium Clock.

EDWARD FRANKLIN – AS MAYOR OF DUNSTABLE

(JS)

This Photograph of Edward Franklin was taken during his many years as a Town Councillor and Mayor. He was Mayor in 1911, 1916 and 1917. He died in 1918 aged 69 years, and therefore did not live to see the post-Great War celebrations in 1919, or the new era ushered in by these events.

The Funeral of Edward Franklin –1918

Frederick Franklin ran an Undertakers business for many years and the family were able to provide a suitably furnished procession befitting the funeral of a celebrated citizen and personality of the town.

The photo opposite shows the splendid cortege with decorated vehicles on its way to the cemetery in West Street, passing the 'White Horse' public house in Church Street where Edward had been the licensee. It would be strange if the long procession following the carriage did not include the Borough (Franklins) Band. A close examination seems to indicate it may be there, unless it headed the procession and was not included in the picture. The 'White Horse' had been the 'headquarters' of the Borough Brass Band since its inception. This ancient building was demolished in the 1960s together with the whole of upper Church Street on the north side to allow for the widening of the cross roads. In the year 2003 the town has the privilege of seeing huge lorries etc thundering through. After Edward's death, Septimus took over the license of the hostelry until 1932.

THE FUNERAL PROCESSION FOR EDWARD FRANKLIN 1918

Septimus Franklin

An interview with Septimus Franklin in the *Dunstable Gazette* of 9th October 1924 describes the discovery of some old papers in the rafters of the 'White Horse' in Church Street, during building work. These were found to be records of the premises, and of licensees' activities, going back to John (1), and his role as Town Constable, and the ensuing era.

DUNSTABLE GAZETTE 9TH OCTOBER 1924

Mr. Franklin, (opposite) now 73, was interviewed and was quoted as 'having lived always at the White Horse and was the current licensee'. He was also 'still playing in the Borough Band, – which probably is the oldest in the county'.

He was looking forward to 'playing around the town for the 61st Christmas in succession'.

Sixty years previously – in 1864 he was sworn in to the Old Volunteer Corps as a drummer-boy, and it was from the band of that corps that the Borough band was formed. (He would have been 13 years of age at that time – Ed.).

The papers recovered during the building works at the 'White Horse' were investigated by a Luton News representative who was called in by Septimus, who then gave the papers to Mr T. W. Bagshawe for the (then) Dunstable museum. The 'Gazette' goes on to say – 'the papers described a different Dunstable from today, (1924), with its endless procession of motor vehicles', remarking that 'a century ago 80 horse-drawn coaches passed through the town, and that in 1818, the population was barely 1300'.

The Funeral of Septimus Franklin – 1932
Septimus Franklin died in 1932 aged 81 years. Septimus (or 'Sep' as Mrs. Stanley, his great-niece calls him), had taken over as Licensee of the 'White Horse' after Edward's death in 1918.

THE FUNERAL PROCESSION FOR SEPTIMUS FRANKLIN 1932

The Cortege was perhaps not as splendid as Edward's in 1918, but it is still an impressive sight with the Borough Band in full attendance. The hearse is horse-drawn but it is followed by motor vehicles as befits the year 1932.

The photo shows the old crossroads, with the 'Red Lion' Hotel at the left of the opening to Church Street where the adjacent building was the 'White Horse' public house, the headquarters of the Band. Most of the buildings in the picture have since been demolished. However, the site on the corner of West St. / High St. South was still there as an Estate Agency in the year 2003 – (formerly 'Keeps' the newsagents).

Septimus was probably the last surviving member of the family to be thus honoured. So far, no further photos have been discovered of the family or band. The band was last mentioned in the town guide of 1939, just seven years later.

The Borough Brass Band from 1932–1940

The photograph of Septimus Franklin's funeral in 1932 (opposite) is the last known in the present archives of the band. The photo shows 14 to16 marching players in step with the music, obviously under the direction of the bandmaster at that time.

The Band was represented at the Silver Jubilee celebrations in Dunstable on 6th May 1935, and was mentioned in the souvenir programme shown in detail in the chapter on the Excelsior Brass Band. The 1937 Guide names the conductor as Mr. F. Duncombe of Church Street, and the secretary as Mr. P. Morgan of Winfield Street. 1937 of course was the year of the coronation of King George VI, and Dunstable's celebrations would have included the Borough Band, although we have no record so far. References to the band continued to appear in the Dunstable Town Guides up to and including 1939, after which there was no further reference.

It can only be assumed that the Old Borough Band became defunct by about 1940. By this time of course the Second World War was taking its toll on the population available to play and celebrate music locally. The Excelsior Band continued to be mentioned, although the numbers available after call up for military service were being reduced, and the Excelsior more or less had to wait for returning servicemen in 1945 / 46 before it could operate as a viable band again.

By the late 1930s there were probably no surviving Franklins in the band. The Franklins still in the Town, and advertising in the 1940/41 Town Guide, included Mr.E. (Edgar) Franklin, – funeral furnisher, carpenter and builder – of 27, Church Street, and Mr. W. J. Franklin, wholesale and retail tobacconist, confectioner, and travel agent, – of 43, High Street North. There was also an Emily Harriet Franklin living at 57, Church Street. Edgar Franklin was the son of Edward, the former mayor as described earlier. Edgar was a bell-ringer at the Priory church but did not play in the band. William Franklin, son of George played in the band – (one of the ten Franklins of three generations to play in the Borough & Volunteer Bands), but it is not certain whether this is the same W. Franklin as referred to above.

So the Franklins & the Old Borough Band, or the 'Beer & Baccy Band', finally bowed out of the musical life of Dunstable after eighty or so years of existence.

5 THE HOUGHTON REGIS BAND

Pictorial evidence of the existence of a Village Band, Brass Band, or similar group in Houghton Regis is at present limited to the single photograph, kindly supplied by Miss Ivy Tompkins of Houghton Regis from her collection of vintage photographs of the village, and shown on the following page. References to 'The Village Band' and the 'Houghton Regis Brass Band' have however appeared from time to time from the mid 1800s, for example, the 'Dunstable Chronicle' reported that 'A Rural Festival was held in July 1856 at which the Brass Band played'.

Another intriguing reference is to be found in The Dunstable Town Guide for 1933, where there is a potted history of the Dunstable Excelsior Silver Prize Band, founded in 1864 as the 'Dunstable Temperance Band'. The article goes on to say that 'it was known by that name until 1885, when the *(Dunstable) Band* amalgamated with the *'Houghton Regis Band'* and became known as the *'Dunstable Promenade Band'*. . . After a short period however the bands separated and the Dunstable Band again took on the name 'Excelsior'.' The Dunstable Promenade Band is interestingly featured on a poster issued in June 1887, advertising events in Dunstable for Queen Victoria's Jubilee.

The geographical boundaries of Houghton Regis have of course changed a good deal over the years, which may confuse the issue from time to time. Much of what is now Dunstable, used to be *'Upper Houghton Regis'*.

The above is a part of an interesting group photo of about fifty men in Houghton Regis, thought to be around the early 20.th C. Seated in the front is a group of younger men, with the two men on the left & far right each holding a drum and sticks – they may perhaps have been part of a band of some kind.

THE HOUGHTON REGIS BRASS BAND IN 1894

(IT)

This rare photograph has been kindly supplied by Miss Ivy Tompkins of Houghton Regis from her collection of vintage photographs of the village. The only person named in the group is Mr. Tompkins senior, Miss Tompkin's grandfather, Percy (born 1873), shown 2nd from Right in the Front Row. The date on the reverse is the year 1894. The site of the photo is not stated, although the densely wooded background may be recognised by older residents.

There are twelve persons in the picture carrying instruments, with another person at the back who may be a collector for the Band. Five of the musicians are wearing a uniform jacket, similar to the Rifle Volunteers although slightly different in design. They are all sporting straw boaters however, and all appear to be wearing a medal or buttonhole on the left side of their jackets.

6 THE DUNSTABLE EXCELSIOR SILVER PRIZE BAND

This chapter on the Excelsior Silver Prize Band is the longest of the book and in fact represents an archive record of the band. It is reliably thought that the foundation date was 1865, the year of the first municipal election following the granting of Dunstable's Charter of Incorporation in 1864. It was founded as a temperance band, and in fact was called the 'Dunstable Temperance Band' – supported by the temperance societies of the neighbourhood – perhaps as a counter to the Borough Band formed about 1860, a year after the re-founding of the Rifle Volunteers in 1859, which body as we have seen had its own band with links to the (Old) Borough Band – also known as the 'Beer & Baccy Band', obviously not a temperance organisation. (We also know from earlier pages that a 'Dunstable Brass Band' was in existence prior to 1856). The band was particularly well known for the seven or more members of the Dolman family who played in its ranks – William Dolman becoming its conductor for several decades. The Borough Band was particularly known for ten members of the Franklin family being involved. In those days, if you were going to have a large family, they might as well form their own brass band as anything else!

The name of the Excelsior Band incorporates 'Silver' – referring to its (eventual) acquisition of silver (plated) instruments, replacing mere 'brass', and 'prize' referring to its successes in brass band contests. The name 'Excelsior' is probably a reference to the standard aimed for by the founders. The band's history spans virtually 100 years from 1865 until a year or two before 1965, by which date the band had been disbanded, not being able to raise an ensemble to play at the Pageant of 1963.

The band nevertheless had a distinguished history of service to the Town and it is hoped the following pages do it justice.

The photograph of the Band (opposite above) was taken c.1898 at the rear of the Ashton Schools, Church Street, and may be the first picture so far available of the Band since its formation in 1865. A similar photo was also taken at the time, but with all the subjects wearing hats! The gentleman 2nd right, bottom row, is Mr. William Dolman, (his hat can be seen under his seat), who succeeded Mr. Eli Inns as Bandmaster in 1898, beginning a long tenure in that role lasting over several decades.

This photograph (opposite below) must be one of the oldest of the vintage Excelsior photos, probably dating to the early 20th C – 1910 has been suggested. The picture has been computer enhanced to remove blemishes. The original was supplied by Mrs. Dolman. The full identification of the members present is still not complete, but members of the Dolman family appear to be there. The gentleman on the left is Mr. Billy Walker who became one of the longest serving members of the band. Mr. Walker is carrying a wad of music and others also are holding their music – except the figure 2nd left. His identity is intriguing – he does not have an instrument and appears to be

THE DUNSTABLE EXCELSIOR SILVER PRIZE BAND – 1898

The names of the 34 people in the picture are: Back row: H.Snoxell, G.Bateman, W.Cleaver, W.Smith, W. Derbyshire, H.Arnold, W.Astling, Art.Dolman, Mr.Carter, Jno.Dolman. Next row: W.Harris, F.Duncombe, A.Duncombe, F.Summerfield, A.Morgan, H.Walker, W.Impey, W.Walker. Third row: L.White, W.Brown, Joe Dolman, E.Walker, Albert Dolman, F. Gibbons, F. Astling, F. Deacon. Front row: Joe.Dolman(Snr), J.Burgess, W.Bull, (Trustees-W.Love, F.T.Garrett-Mayor, T.Burch,) William Dolman, D.King.

THE EXCELSIOR BRASS BAND AT THE TURN OF THE 20TH CENTURY

The occasion could have been a Christmas Carol outing in the snows of winter when Dunstable was a small country town - before it acquired parts of (Upper) Houghton Regis and the area became more industrialised.

dressed in a military uniform: his hat badge may inspire somebody to hazard an informed guess – perhaps he was home on leave from the Boer War which could place the date at around 1902 or before. The rest of the band had not yet acquired band uniforms as such.

THE EXCELSIOR BAND IN 1902

Back Row (L–R): W. Walker, ..., H. Pullen, ..., ..., J. Dolman, B. Seabrook, John Dolman, Albert Dolman, B. Mea, Joe Dolman.
Middle Row (L–R): ...., ..., ..., L. Fountain, W.Bull.
Front Row (L–R): ...., Mr. Duncombe, ..., A. Dolman, William Dolman, ..., ..., ...

The photograph above must have been a popular example as it has turned up in several collections. 1902 appears to be the correct date – its rural setting has not so far been identified, but of course Dunstable was a small country town then and much of the district around was still in fact part of Houghton Regis. The countryside was all around and there was still a farm in the middle of the town. At the feet of W. Dolman and to the left of the 'mascot' can be seen a prize trophy. Many of the musicians have been identified but there are still several as yet not named. Those that have been are listed below. There are 24 in the whole group.

The background to the picture shows a by now old fashioned haystack – the sort that needles used to be lost in, and to the right can be seen a typical item of farm machinery of the era.

A 'Review of Brass Bands in Luton & District' – 1907

This was a slim publication containing information and photographs about a large number of Brass Bands mainly centered on Luton and the area to the east, and which included a history of the *Dunstable Excelsior (Brass) Band*, using the rather quaint language of the time, from which this reference is derived. The author informed his readers that the Excelsior Band was formed about the year 1865 and started as the *Dunstable Temperance Band*. It was supported by the different temperance societies of the neighbourhood. One gentleman in particular, who was a staunch supporter of the band at its commencement, was Mr. Alfred Inwards, who became a J.P. for Dunstable. He was the band's first secretary.

The first bandmaster was Mr. Henry Watson, who was a thorough teetotaller and a good musician. Anyone who wished to join the band would first have to sing or whistle some tune to him, and if they performed the different tests that he set them to do fairly well, then they were admitted members of the band. He had plenty of volunteers for this new band.

'Dunstable people thought a lot of Mr. Watson, and presented him with a silver-plated cornet which he played for over twenty years. He advanced the band remarkably well. They went to a contest taking their drums with them, but the drums were disqualified before they started. Still they played very creditably, but did not come in for a prize'. (At this time, drums were not always considered as a legitimate part of a brass band's line-up.)

Shortly after this the band changed its name to the 'Dunstable Excelsior Band', and also, temporarily, its fortune. It gradually began to go down-hill, and our old and esteemed friend (Mr.Watson) gave way, owing to advancing years, to a younger man by the name of Mr George Richardson. The band at this time was only about seven strong, but they improved a little and got stronger in numbers, and in the year 1895 (c) they persuaded Mr. Eli Inns to become bandmaster.

'He was a good cornet player and a hard worker and soon made improvements, and all the old instruments were got together. Some of these old instruments were very old fashioned, and it required a bit of pluck for some of the bandsmen to appear in public with these out-of-date instruments. One day, Mr. Inns made a journey to Luton and listened to the Luton Town Prize Band rehearsing under Mr. Randolph Ryan, and when he arrived home he talked the matter over with his band, and this was their first step towards professional tuition'.

They eventually engaged the services of Mr. W. Goodger, who persuaded them to get some new instruments. A few were purchased, and these improved the band a lot and they attended the contest at Luton, but were not in the prize list. However, they were not downhearted and their bandmaster, Mr. Inns, kept them well occupied at rehearsals.

After a while they changed conductors, and had the services of Mr. J. T. Ogden as teacher, who persuaded them to attend the Leighton Buzzard Contest. Here they scored for the first time, dividing 3rd and 4th prize with Fenny Stratford. Thence they went to the Woburn Sands Contest and won 3rd prize. They then began to think they could really play a bit!

The next contest they attended was one held in the Plait Hall at Luton. The test piece was 'The Bohemian Girl'. For this event they worked very hard under Mr. Ogden, and they tied with the Luton Red Cross Band, but in the play off for 1st place the Luton band beat them. It is worthy of record that at this contest they had the honour of beating the St. Albans City Band, at that period the champion band of the south, so that the men accomplished a very noteworthy performance.

The Band continued to forge ahead, and Mr Inns began to reap the harvest of his hard work. At the St Albans contest they won two seconds. Shortly after this, Mr. Inns resigned, having laid a good foundation and set a good example to the whole of the bandsmen.

The next gentleman to take charge of the band was the present conductor, Mr. William Dolman, who was elected unanimously by the whole band to the position. The first thing he did was to try and get better instruments, and he persuaded the trustees and members of the band to have a full set of Besson's instruments, which they did. The band attended the Leighton Buzzard contest under the conductorship of Mr. W. Greenwood, and won 4th prize with the test piece, 'Moses in Egypt'.

Then Mr. Dolman conducted them for the first time at a contest, this being at Apsley, with the test piece, 'Gems of Nova Scotia', and they got 4th place again, whilst later they secured two 2nds at St Albans.

Mr. Cooper was engaged as the next conductor, and he took them to several contests, but he only added one prize to their list, and that was a 4th in the Manor House Field, Dunstable. Mr Dolman coached them for the future, and they have never regretted it, for since he had been their teacher, they met with more success than during the whole history of the band at that time.

The following are some of the victories achieved under Mr. Dolman:
Tottenham Contest – divided 1st and 2nd with Hampstead Borough.
Dunstable Contest – divided 1st and 2nd with Luton Red Cross.
Fifth in the Championship of the South at the Crystal Palace.
Second prize and six medals, viz: conductor's medal, tenor horn medal and four
*   medals for the best set of basses on the field, at Walthamstow.*
2nd prize at the Crystal Palace, 1st prize, 10 Guinea Challenge cup, and cornet
*   for the best cornet solo, and euphonium medal at Langford.*

They then had their instruments silver plated at Besson's, and the following year they started contesting again, and won 1st prize and challenge cup and special prize for conductor at Lewisham; 4th prize at Wembley Park in the 1st section; divided 4th prize with Olney band at Berkhamsted; and at the great contest at the Crystal Palace, 1904, they came in tenth.

Then the inhabitants of Dunstable, as a mark of appreciation for what Mr. Dolman had done for the efficiency of the band, presented him with a handsome illuminated address and a silver-mounted baton. Mr. Dolman certainly made Dunstable popular in the brass band world. 'William scored all these victories off his own bat, so to speak, for he had no professional teacher to come behind him to polish up what he had done. He taught the band, took them to concerts and came off victorious'.

'As a musician, Mr. Dolman stands pre-eminent in the Royal Borough of Dunstable. On the occasion of his wedding he was presented with a beautiful

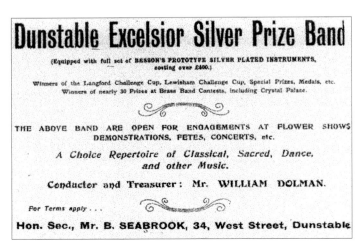

marble clock. He is a staunch teetotaller, and is respected by the bandsmen and all who know him. May the time be long distant when he severs his connection with the Dunstable Band!

'*A word of praise is also due to the whole of the bandsmen who have worked so hard to bring the band up to its present standard (c1906). They delight the inhabitants of Dunstable with capital weekend concerts, and it is suggested that the time is not far off when the Dunstable Town Council should take steps to do something for this band in a practical way. It should be mentioned that Mr. Joseph Dolman, father to the present conductor, is a member of the band, and he has several other sons who are members of this band, and all are good musicians.*'

The 'Review' included several interesting references to the locality and the life of the town in those days, and incorporated the advert for the Band, shown opposite, concluding these extracts from the 'Review of Brass Bands 1907'.

THE EXCELSIOR LEADS A TEMPERANCE MARCH – 1908

The Excelsior Band of 1908 can be seen here in this press cutting, leading a Temperance Drive along High Street North – actually on the wrong side of the carriageway – passing the old buildings at the crossroads, namely the 'Red Lion' on the eastern corner of Church Street, the Home & Colonial shop on the opposite side of Church Street, and other premises now demolished or much altered. The building immediately to the left of the rather large banner was probably the old Post Office.

The Excelsior Band of course was founded by the Temperance Movement's leaders in the Town many years before in 1865, who provided the means of obtaining instruments, music, tuition and practice facilities and so on. It would appear that the musicians in this picture could be wearing a form of uniform, certainly judging by the headgear. They are also well drilled in that they are perfectly in step and are holding the larger instruments at a similar angle. The Band certainly appear to be marching rather than walking and are probably encouraging the procession to keep in step too.

1910 – FUNERAL PROCESSION FOR KING EDWARD V11

The above shows an enlargement of part of a photograph of the funeral procession for the late King Edward VII in Dunstable, featuring the main procession and Band emerging from the Town Hall into High Street North. This picture was at one time wrongly ascribed to the 1919 Peace Celebrations and was included in the 1919 Commemorative booklet published at that time.

It can be seen in the photo that the band is followed by several groups of men in uniform, clearly recognised from this enlargement. Amongst these is a group of young men dressed in a uniform similar to that of the 'Drum-Major' figure leading the procession. They are possibly a contingent of Boys Brigade members to whom the honour of leading the Parade has been given to one of their number, who is seen wearing a sash and carrying a mace in his right hand.

The Excelsior Leads the Fire Brigades of 1911 in their Gala

Whit Monday, June 5th 1911. The occasion was the Annual Fire Brigades competitions of the National Fire Brigades Union (S. Midlands District) held in Dunstable. Fire Crews from Beds., Bucks., Herts., Essex, Northants & North London paraded along High Street North with their horse-drawn engines and wearing their best uniforms and polished helmets on their way to the competition site at a field off Brewers Hill Close. The old buildings form an almost picturesque backdrop to the parade.

In the photograph opposite The Old Sugar Loaf Hotel can plainly be seen at the top left of the picture and the hostelry in the right foreground is thought to

THE FIRE BRIGADES GALA 1911

(DG)

be the 'White Hart', which was later rebuilt and was eventually demolished to make way for the Quadrant shopping centre. A tram can also be seen to the top left (probably horse-drawn). The poster advertising the event promised realistic steamer and manual wet drills, rescues with fire escapes etc, plenty of amusements, and dancing in the evening – tickets no more than 6d (2½p). Dunstable had for many years the oldest fire 'engine' in the country. It was eventually replaced by a brand new one in 1856, when the new machine was purchased by public subscription. The original is still to be seen in a London museum.

South Beds Territorial Recruiting Week 31 May–5 June 1914

Prior to the outbreak of World War One, a Territorial Army recruiting drive was held in Dunstable during the week 31st May–5th June 1914. This was recorded in a Souvenir Booklet which was issued shortly afterwards. This document was a very informative and well illustrated item, containing 12 pages, featuring good quality photographs. It sets out in detail the week's programme of events – Page 1 shown overleaf.

The type and size of font make it difficult to read but it can be seen that all the local organisations of the town were involved and of course both the 'Excelsior' and 'Borough' Bands were prominently featured, probably the last occasion until the Peace Celebrations in 1919. Whatever the future was to hold, this Parade must have been quite impressive – as the narrative says it was 'upwards of ¾ mile in length'. The event incorporated the Whit-Sun Holiday period, and the whole week was marked by parades and meetings. The whole event was commended to the mayor by the Lord Lieutenant as a great success.

As was to be expected, the fire brigades were prominently featured, as the photos overleaf portray.

RECRUITMENT SOUVENIR BOOKLET

The cover page, originally printed on a green background.

INTRODUCTION.

THIS little Booklet is intended as a Souvenir of the Territorial Recruiting Week in Dunstable. The Territorial Forces in the County of Bedford being below strength, the County Authorities were required by the Army Council to bring the Regiment up to strength, and also to provide two additional full Companies, hitherto supplied by Huntingdonshire.

The Lord Lieutenant of Bedfordshire (S. H. Whitbread, Esq.) took up the task and called a meeting of representative men of the southern part of the County at Luton Town Hall, on the 8th of April, 1914. At this Meeting, a Central Executive Committee was formed to organize a Recruiting Campaign in the Southern Division of the County. The Mayor of Luton was appointed Chairman, and Mr. H. Inwards, of Luton, accepted the post of Hon. Secretary. The Mayor of Dunstable was asked to take up the matter, and organize in Dunstable.

He at once called a Meeting at the Town Hall and a strong working Committee was formed, with the Mayor as Chairman, and Councillor C. Hinton as Hon. Secretary. The Recruiting Week had been fixed by the Central Committee for the week May 30th to June 7th, and the local Committee got energetically to work at once. Proceedings commenced on the 11th May when the Army Film was on exhibition at the Picture Palace during the week, Mr. Marchant, the proprietor, admitted all persons in uniform and all Recruits who had joined, free, on Wednesday.

The Committee arranged a rota of speakers, two of whom each evening briefly addressed the audience on the subject of recruiting. Recruits soon began to come in.

The great event was a Church Parade on Whit-Sunday with a Drum Head Service on the Square. The procession extended for upwards of a quarter of a mile, and consisted of the Band of the 5th Battalion of the Beds Regt., followed by the Dunstable Church Lads Brigade Band. Next in order came the 5th Batt., under the command of Major Brighten, followed by over 100 recruits. Colonel Butler, Commanding Officer of the Battalion, was also in attendance. The Grammar School Cadets followed. Then came about 110 National Reservists. The Dunstable Church Lads Brigade and the Houghton Regis Company followed next in order. The Dunstable, Houghton Regis and Markyate Fire Brigades, with the Excelsior Band, headed the Civic procession, consisting of the Mace Bearer, the Mayor, in his robes, and the Corporation, the Magistrates and Officials, and representative prominent local gentlemen. These were followed by the Dunstable Troop of Girl Guides, the Dunstable and Kensworth Boy Scouts, and contingents of the various Friendly Societies, headed by the Borough Band. The Scouts Band brought up the rear of what was a most imposing procession.

The Military Section detrained and formed up at the L. & N.W. Station. The Civic procession marshalled in George Street and Park Street, under the able control of Mr. J. W. Vernon and a staff of assistants, fell in behind the Military and marched to the Square where a Drum Head Service was conducted by the Rev. W. W. C. Baker, Chaplain to the 5th Beds, assisted by the Rev. F. C. Mahony and the Rev. E. Lucas. The Lord Lieutenant of the County, accompanied by Colonel de Winton, commanding the East Midland Brigade, unexpectedly arrived upon the scene, just at the moment the Civic procession was entering the military square, and at the end of the Service took the salute from the troops.

(1)

Page One.

The Town was bedecked with flags and banners, and the local 'Luton Reporter' newspaper reported enthusiastically on Dunstable's efforts. Events also took place on the Downs, the Waterlows sports ground, & the town hall as well as in Leighton Buzzard and Luton. A 'snapshot' of one of the bands (opposite below) was included in the booklet – it is probably one of the Military Bands – e.g. the Band of the 5th Battalion of the Bedfordshire Regiment, as mentioned in the Introduction above. The Booklet included photos of the Grammar School Cadets, Dunstable & Houghton Regis G.L.B., Dunstable Girl Guides, and Dunstable Scouts – but did not feature the Brass Bands – in fact the only 'band' picture was of the 5th Battalion (?) opposite.

RECRUITMENT SOUVENIR BOOKLET, THE FIRE BRIGADES

DUNSTABLE AND HOUGHTON REGIS FIRE BRIGADES.

SERGEANTS OF "B" (DUNSTABLE) COMPANY.

The brigade in the third picture is Markyate & Flamstead.

The Band of the 5th Battalion of the Bedfordshire Regiment (?)

After The Great War – Peace celebrations in 1919

Although photographs at the time were in black and white (other than if they were tinted afterwards), we should bear in mind there was a great deal of colour to be seen everywhere in the town on these occasions, with flags, bunting across the streets, arches, signs, etc. (more perhaps than might be seen today), along with the extensive processions, with the bands and their various uniforms, with everybody waving Union Jacks and hanging drapes from the windows of private houses, and from public and other buildings.

THE 19TH JULY PEACE CELEBRATIONS SOUVENIR PROGRAMME

The Title Page of the Peace Celebrations Souvenir Programme was in colour. Inside was a 20 page booklet of reports of everything that took place, with complimentary testimonials and many photographs.

PEACE CELEBRATIONS COMMEMORATIVE CUP

The above are the obverse and reverse views taken from the commemorative cup issued nationally in July 1919, with the individual town's name printed in black – (perhaps by local firms).

PEACE CELEBRATION REVEILLES

A series of Reveilles, starting outside the Town Hall at 6.30 a.m., the Scouts and Grammar School buglers combining. Afterwards this was to be repeated at various parts of the Town – no late risers were permitted that day!

MORE FROM THE PEACE CELEBRATIONS PROGRAMME 1919

PROGRAMME OF MUSIC

BY THE

Dunstable Excelsior Silver Prize Band

(Conductor, Mr. W. DOLMAN).

oooooooo

MARCH ...	" Bravest of the Brave "		*George Gay.*
SELECTION	" Top of the Bill " (On Popular Songs).	...	*S. Baker.*
VALSE ...	" Satanique "		*A. Trevelyn.*
MARCH ...	" Land of Hope and Glory"		*Elgar.*
SELECTION	" Dawn of Victory " (On Popular Songs).		*E. Pether.*
VALSE ...	" Ecstacy "		*Sydney Baynes.*
... ...	" Menai Bells "	...	*Senogles.*
MARCH ...	" Freedom and Honour "		*Rimmer.*
SELECTION	" Rusticus "	...	*Allan.*
MORCEAU	" Pomona "	...	*Douglas.*

oooooooo

Programme subject to Alteration.

Page nineteen on the left sets out the Excelsior Band's programme of music. 'Land of Hope and Glory' is certainly recognisable today – but how many in the rest of the list would be recognised today is doubtful.

The order is repeated throughout, ie. March–Selection–Valse (other than 'morceau', which must simply mean 'piece').

The programme also contained this photo (below) of the Priory bellringers, with their names.

The group includes: Canon Baker & Messrs – F Baldock, E. Franklin, F. Franklin, S. Franklin, R. Harris, G. Heley, W. Horne, C. E. King, C. T. King, C. King, H. Matthews, F. Ramsey, A. Sharman, and in the foreground two of the scouts/ringers who sounded the Reveille, A. Pratt & P. Ward.

Below: This part of the grand procession is seen approaching the town centre from High Street South, with the Square in the background. The line of buildings still has a familiar form to this day, although many changes have been made. The telegraph pole is near to where the Millennium Clock has been erected, and the improvements of 2002. The procession was of great length and included a wide range of organisations from the town.

THE EXCELSIOR IN PROCESSION IN THE PEACE CELEBRATIONS 1919

(HCM)

The section of the Square behind the tableau wagon following the Band is an interesting feature which has so far eluded identification but looks like a section of the cattle market in which there appears to be a number of people and perhaps stalls of some description.

The Excelsior can clearly be seen leading this part of the procession, and the band was kept very busy the whole day, which lasted from 6.30 a.m. to 11.45 p.m. and later, ending with a tableau on the Town Hall balcony. The photo was featured in the Peace Celebrations Programme.

THE SCOUTS IN PROCESSION AT THE JULY 19TH 1919 PEACE CELEBRATIONS

(MM

This photo shows the local Boy Scouts drum and bugle band leading part of the procession past the southern approaches to the 'Square'. The procession seems to have stopped at this point – perhaps to acknowledge a group of spectators seated on a dais behind the tree on the right of the picture. The band is certainly still playing although halted. It is quite probable that the Scouts are a combined group of the various local troops in Dunstable.

Two other privately taken scenes are shown here.

(MM)

None of these photographs appears in the Peace Celebrations Programme.

END OF WORLD WAR 1 – A VIGIL ON THE DOWNS

(MM)

The occasion features a tableau with local children taking part and is flanked by soldiers on guard, heads bowed. The crowd includes guides & civic dignitaries.

RAMC DUNSTABLE CAMP 1919

(MM)

Three musicians of the RAMC in the front row may be part of a larger Army Band, (on the left a clarinet, in the middle a bugle, on the right a cornet).

WATERLOW'S SPORTS GROUND 1923

(M[

Members of the 'Excelsior' pose for the camera during a pause in their programme at the Waterlow & Sons sports ground in 1923. The band members are not wearing uniform which they invariably did later on – flat caps and boaters are the order of the day here, with an occasional trilby. The lines of palings suggest some athletic activities, and we may assume it is sometime during the summer season. Union jacks can be seen being flown from the pavilion which might indicate the occasion as Empire Day.

The pavilion at the ground was large enough to accommodate dances and social events as well as the necessary changing rooms etc for sporting events. Waterlow's own dance band 'WASSO' (Waterlow & Sons Athletic, Sports & Social Association Orchestra), frequently played for dances there (as did other dance bands). The premises were often hired by other organisations in the town also.

The printing firm had its own football and cricket teams of course for many years, as well as its own bands, being a major employer in Dunstable over several decades until the 1980s or so. In the firm's earlier days, it was said that ability in sports or music could often get you a job with the Company!

1924 – THE EXCELSIOR IN DR LATHBURY'S GARDEN

(JB)

A well balanced pose on this occasion in 1924, in the garden of Dr. Lathbury in West Street showing off their Trophy collection. 'The Limes' was a frequent backdrop for the Band as for other Dunstable organisations.

Dr Lathbury & his family were well respected in the town over many years and often made their extensive premises available to the townspeople, situated as they were then near to the Dunstable crossroads and extending back to the area to the rear, shielded from the older buildings behind by trees and shrubs, not far from where the Wesleyan Institute was situated and the building where the Excelsior practised for some years.

Some by now familiar figures are to be seen, one or two long serving veterans included, with Mr. S.J.Darby and William Dolman seated centre with the shield and baton.

TWO CONCERT PROGRAMMES – 1928 *the front pages (above) and back pages (below) – half size*

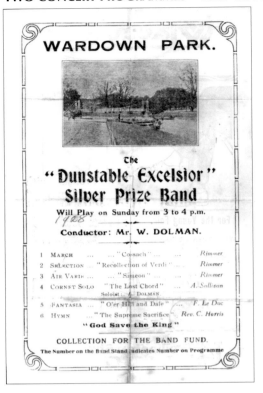

WARDOWN PARK.

The
**"Dunstable Excelsior"
Silver Prize Band**

Will Play on Sunday from 3 to 4 p.m.

1928

Conductor: Mr. W. DOLMAN.

1	MARCH	...	"Cossack"	...	*Rimmer*
2	SELECTION	"Recollection of Verdi"	...	*Rimmer*
3	AIR VARIE	...	"Simeon"	...	*Rimmer*
4	CORNET SOLO	"The Lost Chord"	...	*A. Sullivan*

Soloist : — DOLMAN.

| 5 | FANTASIA | ... | "O'er Hill and Dale" | ... | *F. Le Duc* |
| 6 | HYMN | ... | "The Supreme Sacrifice" | *Rev. C. Harris* |

"God Save the King"

COLLECTION FOR THE BAND FUND.

The Number on the Band Stand indicates Number on Programme

**The Gardens of
"The Limes" West St.**

June 1928

The
**"Dunstable Excelsior"
Silver Prize Band**

Will play on Sunday at 7-30 p.m.

Conductor : MR W. DOLMAN.

1	March	...	"El Dorado"	...	*J. A. Greenwood*
2	Overture	...	"Pique Dame"	*Franz Von Suppe*
3	Suite	...	"Bohemian"	(A Gipsy Love Story)
					J. Ord Hume

1. The Appeal.   2. The Caravan
3. Tarantella.

4	Fantasia	"A Military Church Parade"	*J. Ord Hume*
5	March	...	"Militaire No. 1."	...	*F. Shubert*
6	Hymn	"The Supreme Sacrifice"	*Rev. C. Harris*

"God Save The King"

COLLECTION FOR THE BAND FUND.

Parsons, Printer, Dunstable.

A Portrait of William Dolman – Bandmaster & Conductor

William Dolman was one of nine of his family to play in the 'Excelsior' Brass Band – himself, his father and seven brothers – only one short of the ten Franklins in the Borough Band.

They also participated regularly in the Bible Class Orchestra. William in fact came to conduct both at times, becoming particularly well-known as conductor of The 'Excelsior' Silver Prize Band over a long and successful period.

This portrait comes from a segment of a 1910 photograph of the Bible Class Orchestra.

He won many honours in the Band contest field including a conductor's medal. He was also conductor of the West Street Baptist Choir, the Three Arts Society Orchestra, the Totternhoe Choral Society, and others in what was to be a long career in amateur music in the district. His family owned a hat-blocking business in Burr Street in a building (long since demolished) near the pathway to Bennett's Recreation ground. They were also connected with a polish manufacturing business nearby, which became defunct many years ago. William was also featured in the 'Gazette' of the late 'twenties – early 'thirties in the 'Among the Notables' series. This incorporated a cartoon carricature and write-up on a number of well-known Dunstablians including other musicians. William was no. 27 as set out on the following page.

Wm. Dolman – 'AMONG THE NOTABLES' – NO. 27. Dunstable Gazette 1928–32

Mr. William Dolman, another of Dunstable's well-known musicians, whose ability as bandmaster of the Dunstable Excelsior Silver Prize Band should not in any way be "minim"-ised, even at the risk of making his contemporaries a little "crotchety" and causing them to "quaver." For he has blazoned Dunstable's name in the world of music, and so far as his association with the band is concerned, he has become an old and time-honoured institution. The secret of his success as bandmaster is that he is very human, and his lively interest in the well-being of his colleagues earns for him their admiration, co-operation and respect, even though in the ranks of the Excelsior his title is invariably "Bill." He disdains any other.

Born at Breaston, Derbyshire, Mr. Dolman has resided in Dunstable since he was two years of age. When quite young he began to reveal indications of musical talent, and at the early age of eleven came before the bandmaster of the Dunstable Temperance Band, Mr. Henry Watson, for a test in the form of a whistling solo—Mr. Watson's method of discovering whether candidates had an ear for music. Young "Bill" Dolman evidently demonstrated that he had plenty of lung power as well, for he was handed a cornet as reward—not, of course, from the ice cream stall—and it was with this instrument that he soon showed himself as a very useful member of the band.

A few years later the Temperance Band changed its title to the Excelsior, and the fortunes of the band also changed—unfortunately, to its detriment. Mr. Eli Inns, however, succeeding to the bandmastership in the nineties, persuaded the band to procure new instruments and engage professional tuition, and there was a vast improvement in consequence.

Having laid a good foundation, Mr. Inns resigned, and Mr. Dolman was unanimously appointed to the command. He infused a new spirit into its members by training them for competitive work, and the band, after an unprofitable visit to Luton, secured their first award at Leighton Buzzard. After their initial success, which was under the conductorship of the professional tutor, Mr. W. Goodger, the baton was wielded at all contests by Mr. Dolman, and very rare were the occasions when Dunstable Excelsior Band returned home without an award. One very notable occasion for the Excelsior was when they shared first place with the Luton Red Cross Band—who held the championship of the South—when the bands were opposed at Dunstable Park. Other meritorious performances by the band, when Mr. Dolman received trophies on their behalf, include their successes at St. Albans, Little Brickhill, Crystal Palace, Earl's Court, Tottenham, Wembley, Hampstead, Watford, Luton, Fenny Stratford, Letchworth, Dartford and Walthamstow. Twice he has secured conductor's medals.

While the welfare of the Excelsior Band is his principal concern, it does not entirely occupy his leisure hours. For over twenty years Mr. Dolman has been conductor of the Wesleyan Bible Class Orchestra, and was conductor of the Totternhoe Choral Society for three seasons. One of the happiest periods of his life was spent at the West-street Baptist Church, where for fifteen years he was choirmaster. Under his guidance the festivals and anniversaries were particularly happy affairs.

Another string to Mr. Dolman's bow is the Dunstable Three Arts Club's musical directorship, and in every production, with one exception, he has held the baton. The exception was on the occasion when he assisted on the string bass—an instrument which he has watched grow up from a small violin—and on which he performs creditably.

A very keen gardener, Mr. Dolman has proved a very successful exhibitor, and on one occasion, at Leagrave, secured eighteen prizes from twenty exhibits. It is incorrect, however, to say that he obtains such good results by coercing the vegetables to spring up by playing to them on the cornet or string bass after the manner of an Indian snake-charmer.

It was a fitting tribute to his ability that in 1902 the town should present him with a silver-mounted baton and illuminated address, handed him by the then Mayor, Alderman J. Langridge. He was also presented with a handsome marble timepiece on the occasion of his marriage. These were just two incidents that demonstrated the regard in which he is held by his fellow townsmen and colleagues, all of whom appreciate the skill with which he has guided and guarded the interests of the band throughout the thirty years he has been its conductor. In the annals of the Excelsior Band the name of Dolman will always be prominent, not only because of the ability of its conductor, but for the reason that so many members of the family have been connected with it. At one period Mr. Dolman's father and seven brothers wore the Excelsior uniform, and were, moreover, accomplished musicians.

The caricature is attributed to 'HOW' and was accompanied by the write-up above.

DOLMANS' HAT BLOCKING FACTORY c.1930

(MD)

The men in the picture are not all so far fully identified, but the third from left does look like Mr. William Dolman and the fourth right looks like another member of the Dolman family. The premises are long since gone, along with the business, having occupied a site near to the alley way to Bennett's Recreation ground on the west side of Burr Street for a long period. Several of the family have lived in Burr Street for many years.

The Dolmans, Joseph in particular, were also involved with another local business, namely Messrs. Smith & Dolman in St. Mary's Street, making polishing cloths.

The Aylesbury Band Contest 11th June 1932

The Band is pictured opposite after an important contest win at Aylesbury on Saturday 11th of June 1932, proudly displaying the Prize trophies, two cups and the Contest Shield on which their name will be added to the other distinguished winners of the past. Arthur Clarke (Middle row, 2nd right), won the cup for the best trombone at the contest.

Holding the Shield is Mr. William Dolman, Conductor of the Excelsior. The background to the photograph is again the garden of Dr. Lathbury's house ('The Limes') in West Street Dunstable. The original Contest Programme has been preserved and the main sections are set out on the following pages.

THE AYLESBURY CONTEST PROGRAMME, FRONT PAGE – *quarter size*

AYLESBURY PRINTING WORKS
SILVER BAND.

(Hazell's Social and Sports Club).

Programme of Fifth Annual

BAND CONTEST

(Under the Rules of the London and Home Counties Amateur Band Association).

SPORTS AND FETE

Saturday, June 11th, 1932.   From 1-30 to 11.

TO BE HELD ON

Hazell's Social and Sports

:: :: Club Ground. :: ::

Price 2d.

Hon. Secretary—
EDWARD PERROTTET.

Once again, fire brigades feature in the Contest, with Aylesbury and Boxmoor mentioned. It was perhaps a little unexpected that the Band was in the 2nd division, but the Excelsior was nevertheless up against another 6 bands with 2 or 3 from London.

The trophy for Marching & Deportment was the 'Ladies' Challenge Cup. A march of 200 yards does not seem a great distance, but to maintain a high standard of deportment and playing would have needed much rehearsal and concentration. Earlier on, all the bands had to march from the station to the sports ground and play en route, and after the contest play as part of the massed bands taking part. It is perhaps particularly indicative of the values of the time that the money prizes were 2 pounds & 1 pound sterling respectively. During the interval it is a little odd to see 'Aquatic Cock Fighting by members of Hazell's swimming club'!

1932 – THE EXCELSIOR CELEBRATES ANOTHER CONTEST TRIUMPH

(MD/ CS)

The musicians and associates in the picture are: Back Row (L–R): Mr. Fountain, ..., Bert Duncan, Art Dolman, Eric Bell, Jim Bull, Bill Matthews, Bert Poulton. Middle Row (L–R): Joe Dolman, Len Fountain, Sid Fountain, Cecil Tomkins, Art Philpot, Fred Janes, Alb. Dolman, Art Clarke, Sid Butcher. Front Row (L–R): Percy London, Bill Wright, Bert Saunders, Sid Darby, Dr.Lathbury, William Dolman, John Burgess, Harry Lovell, Billy Walker, Wally Harris.

THE TIMETABLE AND THE MARCH & DEPORTMENT CONTEST SHOWING TWO DIVISIONS

BAND CONTEST JOINT COMMITTEE, 1932.

Chairman: Mr. C. L. GREY.
Hon. Treasurer: Mr. F. E. PIPER.
Hon. Secretary: Mr. E. PERROTTET.

Mr. T. R. Walker	Mr. A. Newnes	Mr. W. H. English
,, L. G. White	,, C. Baldwin	,, E. Keedle
,, H. A. Lacey	,, H. Ashurst	,, L. Beechey
,, W. Smith	,, G. Holland	,, W. Birtchnell
,, J. Cheshire	,, G. Feasey	,, H. P. Cowley
,, J. Warner	,, W. Harvey	,, J. Baker
,, G. Edwards	,, E. Bridges	Miss Mundle
,, W. Carr	,, I. Spedding	Mr. W. B. Little

ELECTRICAL EFFECTS BY W. H. ADAMS AND A. FINCHER.

TO-DAY'S TIME TABLE.

(Approximate):

1.30 p.m.—Gates open.
1.30 p.m.—Athletic Procession through the Town
2—3.30 p.m.—Bands will assemble at the L.M.S. Station, High Street, and march at intervals to the Sports Ground, playing en route.
2 p.m.—Michael Beaumont, M.P., will take Olympic Salute on Sports Ground.
2.10 p.m.—Bucks County Elementary Schools' Sports.
3.30 p.m.—Ballot for order of play for Band Contest on Bandstand.
3.45 p.m.—2nd Division Band Contest commences.
5.30 p.m.—March and Deportment Contest, Division I. and Division II.
6.30 p.m.—1st Division Band Contest commences.
7.15 p.m.—Aquatic Cock Fighting by members of Hazell's Swimming Club.
8 p.m.—Massed Bands Performance, consisting of Competing Bands, and Aylesbury Printing Works Band, under the Conductorship of J. A. Greenwood, Birkenhead.
8.15 p.m.—Adjudicators' Awards and Presentation of Prizes by Mrs. O. V. Viney.
8.30 p.m.—Push Ball Match: Aylesbury Town Fire Brigade v. St. John Ambulance (Aylesbury). Referee: Mr. T. B. Rooke.
8.45 p.m.—GRAND GALA DANCE with Illuminations in the Enclosure Music by Aylesbury Printing Works Silver Band.
9.30 p.m.—Draw for Contest Fund Vouchers.
9.45 p.m.—Dance continued.
11 p.m.—Good-night and thank you for your support.

THE MARCH & DEPORTMENT CONTEST.

Adjudicators—Capt. MICHAEL BEAUMONT, M.P.
R.S.M. OLDER, Bucks Batt. O.B.L.I.

This will take place on the Sports Ground (Cricket Pitch) and Bands will be required to march a distance of about 200 yards. This Contest will be decided during an interval between Division I. and II.

DIVISION I.

First Prize: "ADKINS" CHALLENGE CUP and £2 cash.
Second Prize: £1 cash.

1. BARNET TOWN
2. CROYDON BOROUGH
3. FRIARY BREWERY, GUILDFORD
4. HANWELL SILVER
5. ST. PANCRAS SILVER

DIVISION II.

First Prize: "LADIES" CHALLENGE CUP and £2 cash.
Second Prize: £1 cash.

6. BERKHAMSTED EXCELSIOR
7. BOXMOOR BRIGADE
8. DUNSTABLE EXCELSIOR
9. EALING TOWN
10. HOUSE OF DICKINSON
11. LEYTON BOROUGH
12. TOTTENHAM TOWN

THE CONTEST PIECES AND SCORE SHEET

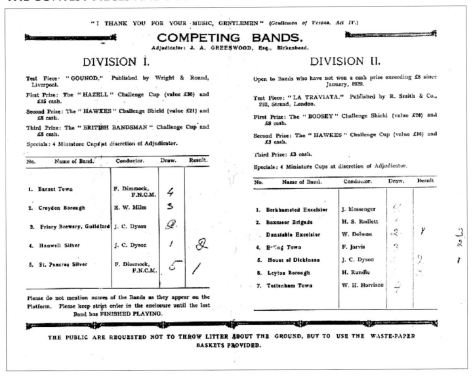

"I THANK YOU FOR YOUR MUSIC, GENTLEMEN" *(Gentlemen of Verona, Act IV.)*

COMPETING BANDS.
Adjudicator: J. A. GREENWOOD, Esq., Birkenhead.

DIVISION I.

Test Piece: "GOUNOD." Published by Wright & Round, Liverpool.

First Prize: The "HAZELL" Challenge Cup (value £30) and £15 cash.

Second Prize: The "HAWKES" Challenge Shield (value £21) and £8 cash.

Third Prize: The "BRITISH BANDSMAN" Challenge Cup and £5 cash.

Specials: 4 Miniature Cups at discretion of Adjudicator.

No.	Name of Band.	Conductor.	Draw.	Result.
1.	Barnet Town	F. Dimmock, F.N.C.M.	4	
2.	Croydon Borough	E. W. Miles	3	
3.	Priory Brewery, Guildford	J. C. Dyson	2	
4.	Hanwell Silver	J. C. Dyson	1	2
5.	St. Pancras Silver	F. Dimmock, F.N.C.M.	5	1

Please do not mention names of the Bands as they appear on the Platform. Please keep strict order in the enclosure until the last Band has FINISHED PLAYING.

DIVISION II.

Open to Bands who have not won a cash prize exceeding £8 since January, 1929.

Test Piece: "LA TRAVIATA." Published by R. Smith & Co., 210, Strand, London.

First Prize: The "BOOSEY" Challenge Shield (value £70) and £8 cash.

Second Prize: The "HAWKES" Challenge Cup (value £14) and £5 cash.

Third Prize: £3 cash.

Specials: 4 Miniature Cups at discretion of Adjudicator.

No.	Name of Band.	Conductor.	Draw.	Result
1.	Berkhamsted Excelsior	J. Messenger	6	
2.	Boxmoor Brigade	H. S. Radlett	1	
	Dunstable Excelsior	W. Dolman	2	3
4.	Belling Town	F. Jarvis	3	2
5.	House of Dickinson	J. C. Dyson	5	
6.	Leyton Borough	H. Rundle		
7.	Tottenham Town	W. H. Harrison	4	1

THE PUBLIC ARE REQUESTED NOT TO THROW LITTER ABOUT THE GROUND, BUT TO USE THE WASTE-PAPER BASKETS PROVIDED.

THE BACK PAGE

APPRECIATION.

The Contest Committee wish most sincerely to acknowledge the kindness of the General Council of Hazell's Social and Sports Club for the use of the Sports Ground, also the generosity of A. T. Adkins, Esq., in presenting a Challenge Cup for annual competition in Division I. of the March and Deportment Contest.

We would take this opportunity of placing upon record our appreciation and thanks to subscribers to the Prize Fund, the London and Home Counties Amateur Bands' Association and its officers, the St. John Ambulance Brigade, and the numerous voluntary helpers who have given their time and abilities to the organisation of our Band Contest and Fete.

To the "Daily Mail" for the loan of the Radio Van and Push Ball. To all Bands who have assisted us to-day with their entry and to their supporters, we extend a hearty welcome, and lastly the Committee THANK YOU for your patronage, and trust that our efforts to interest and amuse you have been successful.

AYLESBURY PRINTING WORKS SILVER BAND

(Licensed by the Performing Right Society, Ltd.)

Affiliated to the

LONDON AND HOME COUNTIES AMATEUR BANDS' ASSOCIATION,

OXFORD AND DISTRICT BAND ASSOCIATION,

BERKS, OXON AND BUCKS GUILD.

Give frequent CONCERTS on this Sports Ground on Sunday evenings, when the General Public are admitted free.

THE NEXT CONCERTS WILL BE GIVEN ON

SUNDAY, JUNE 19th, at 7.30 p.m.

SUNDAY, JUNE 26th, at 7.30 p.m.

The above Band is open for ENGAGEMENTS at Flower Shows, Athletic Sports, Fetes, Concerts, Galas, etc.

While the 'Ladies' Challenge Cup was for Marching & Deportment, the music performance was to be rewarded with, in the case of Division II, the 'Boosey Challenge Shield', for the best rendition of *La Traviata*.

This time the cash prizes were a little more sustantial, even for those days, i.e. £8, £5, & £3, respectively.

Score marks can just be made out on the sheet above. The comments at the foot of the left hand page indicate that this copy might have been used by one of the organisers or perhaps more likely as a check sheet by a band member.

The rest of the programme advertises the Bucks County Elementary Schools Sports, listing all the events and a table in which to record the results. Commercial adverts also feature, as would be expected, referring particularly to products associated with such an event.

Left: The Aylesbury Band, as the host, did not take part, although they were a worthy band in their own right.

1st Dunstable Town Guide 1933

The 1st Dunstable Town Guide, published in 1933, included an article on the history of the Excelsior Band (author unknown). It covered many of the facts included in the 1907 booklet with additional information ie. the Band was founded in the year 1864, and was then known as the Dunstable Temperance Band, its bandmaster being Mr Henry Watson. After a considerable time it was decided to change the title to 'Excelsior', and the band was known by this name until the year 1885, when it amalgamated with Houghton Regis Band and was known as the *'Dunstable Promenade Band'*, (this title appears on an 1887 Queen Victoria Jubilee poster in Dunstable), continuing for a short period when the Bands then separated again. (It should be remembered that a large part of what is now Dunstable was in 'Upper Houghton Regis' until 1907, which may have been a factor in the situation).

'After many years under Bandmasters George Richardson and Eli Inns, the band decided to go in for contesting, professional tuition was engaged and new instruments were bought. The first contest attended was at Luton, but without success. The next contest attended was at Leighton Buzzard, when fourth prize was won. In the year 1898 Mr Eli Inns resigned the Bandmastership and Mr W Dolman was appointed as his successor, the position which he held continuously for many years'.

'During the 35 years up to 1933, under Mr Dolman the band won a large number of prizes and honours at contests, viz., Apsley, Aylesbury, Bedford, Berkhamsted, Camberwell, Crystal Palace, Dartford, Dunstable, Earls Court, Great Brickhill, Langford, Luton, Lewisham, Letchworth, St Albans, Toddington, Tottenham, Walthamstow, Wembley and Woburn. In addition to winning honours as a band its soloists have won medals for solo playing. Mr Joe Dolman (euphonium), 5 medals; Mr Arthur Dolman (solo cornet), gold medal; Messrs. Frank Lay, W.Impey and A. Clarke (solo trombone), silver cup. Medals have also been won by the bass players, for the best set of basses, and a conductor's medal by Mr. Dolman'.

It repeats that Mr. Dolman's activities were not only confined to the Excelsior, he was also Conductor of the West Street Baptist Choir, 15 years; Wesleyan Bible Class Orchestra, 20 years; Three Arts Society Orchestra, 6 years; Totternhoe Choral Society, 4 years. He has also been an arranger of music for Brass Bands or Orchestra. For the past few years to 1933 the band organised its own hospital effort, and was instrumental in raising money to aid many local hospitals. (This was before the 'L&D' was built).

The article was very informative, albeit including some information already detailed on previous pages, but the reference to the 'Houghton Regis Band' is possibly the only reference so far, since the 1856 'Chronicle' report. (Ed.)

The Silver Jubilee of King George V & Queen Mary May 6th 1935

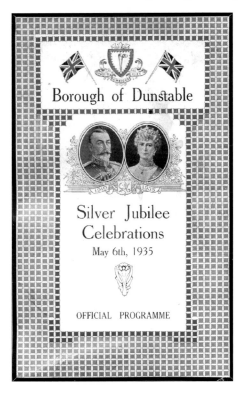

The occasion of a Royal Celebration was always well marked in Dunstable and the Silver Jubilee of 1935 was no exception. The front page of the Official Programme is shown here.

The day's programme started with a peal of bells at the Priory Church at 7.00 a.m, a 21 Gun Salute at 10.30a.m. Divine Service on the Rec. at 11.00 a.m.(Bennett's Rec. is assumed).

At 1.00 p.m. a Lunch for 200 old people at the Town Hall, and a Grand Carnival starting at 6.00 in the evening. Dunstable's three Bands, the Excelsior Silver Prize Band, the Borough Band and the Dunstable Salvation Army Band were strongly represented.A specially composed Jubilee March was played several times during the day by the Excelsior Band.

Dunstable's Fire Station

The picture opposite from 'The Gazette' was taken in January 1939 and shows a contingent from The Excelsior Band playing at the grand opening of the (then) new Fire Station in the purpose-built building next to the entrance to Grove House Gardens. The photo shows the Mayor and other dignitaries conducting the opening ceremony – at this point the band is probably playing a hymn or perhaps the National Anthem. The conductor is almost sure to be Mr. W. Dolman with a dozen musicians, attired in their uniforms. Three policemen can be seen mid-picture and we can see that most of the assembled company are wearing hats and greatcoats, not just because it is winter (snow can be seen in the grounds of the Park and the Grammar School to the left), but it was the dress of the day in 1939. It may be worth noting that the caption to the published photo did not in fact mention the band. Perhaps it had become taken for granted! Inside the building can be seen a fire engine, typical of the design of its day, and the large folding doors drawn back which would allow two engines to be deployed.

After the war, the Fire Station was eventually transferred to its present site at the junction with Brewers Hill Road, after a period at the old CO-OP site in the town centre. The old Station was then used as the Town's Ambulance Station for many years, when this in turn moved elsewhere; and from the year 2000 the building has been used as a young people's centre, now called 'The Place'. It is also used for dispensing refreshments to the crowds attending the Sunday Band

THE 'PLACE' FOR THE 'EXCELSIOR' IN JANUARY 1939

Dunstable's New Fire Station is opened.

Concerts in the Gardens, which now take place on the magnificent new Millennium Bandstand just behind it. The gates in the photo overleaf are in fact part of the original, more ornate set in High Street North which were replaced in recent years after the fabric had deteriorated and become beyond repair.

The Millennium Bandstand site is the third to be occupied by a bandstand in Grove House Gardens. The first was a circular rockery behind the green to the rear of the offices sometimes referred to as 'the Cakestand', and which still can be seen today; the second was another purpose-built design at the rear of the Gardens near the depot area, and which was demolished due to lack of use, in the 1960s, (see later picture). To the right of the 'Place' is a small car park still in use today; however in the earlier days of the building, to the rear of this area was sited the Town Mortuary – not to worry, that is no longer there either!

The new Bandstand has replaced the tented accommodation previously used in Priory Gardens until 2000 and has proved a great success. It is a sad irony however that Dunstable no longer has the 'Excelsior' or a Town Band as such, but the arena has been put to good use by bands from Dunstable schools and of course the many other local and out of town bands, orchestras etc who have entertained the people of Dunstable & district during the extensive programme of events that the Town Council and the sponsors have organised in the Millennium summer 2000 and annually since.

The fire service has featured prominently in the civic history of the Town as exemplified by the 1911 gala (qv) though the above occasion in 1939 was the last to include a brass band. The photo could possibly be the last to be taken of the Band before the beginning of the 1939–45 war. It is worth remembering that neither the Excelsior nor the Borough Band were official bodies in spite of the latter's title. The Excelsior, like the Borough Band, was an unpaid amateur voluntary organisation and never subsidised from the public purse. Many people have expressed surprise at a lack of official public recognition during the Band's long existence. The post-war demise of our local town bands has meant that no similar civic musical participation occurred in 'later' events such as the opening of the Recreation Centre or the Queensway Hall.

The Excelsior Silver Prize Band in 1949

The picture below is the original photograph used on the front page of the programme for the Town Hall Concert on 27th November 1949. The band members in uniform total 29 in all, with 3 persons in 'civvies'. The elegant backdrop to the picture is the back elevation of Priory House. This could be the first photo of the Band after the war and Jim Bull (conductor) tells us that their uniforms were in fact old police uniforms with added braid sewn on, but with new caps. The original photo was provided by Jim Bull, and he was able to identify all but two or three of the people in the photo, as listed below:

THE BAND IN 1949

Back Row – Left to Right: Messrs. Tomkins, R. Williams, R. Janes, D. Parsons, G. Ashby, B. Poulton, J. Creasy, W. Mathews, C. Garget, A. Stanbridge, Mr. Philpott, T. Cook.
Middle Row – Left to Right: Messrs. Hutchins, C. Young, W. Marshall, P. Lawrence, L. Dawson, F. Janes, Mr. Philpott, C. ...., C. Watts, J. Irving, B. Stripp, K. Bayliss, ...
Front Row – Left to Right: P London, W. Walker, Mr. Wesley, J.Bull Conductor, Mr. Stan ...., J.Jenkins.
Front – centre (seated): Ray Parsons.

AN EXCELSIOR CONCERT PROGRAMME AT THE TOWN HALL 27TH NOVEMBER 1949

The Programme, printed in green on yellow, was a comparatively de luxe document but the object was to launch a series of concerts to entertain the public and dignitaries of the Town, to promote the Band, and raise funds for new instruments.

Right: the front page.

Below: the centre pages. The repertoire is fairly varied, with songs performed by Miss Elsie Hewson and Mr. J. Heady making a contrast to the band numbers. Mr. S. J. Darby has been involved with the Band for a great many years as a non-playing administrator having been Secretary for a long time but now described as the President.

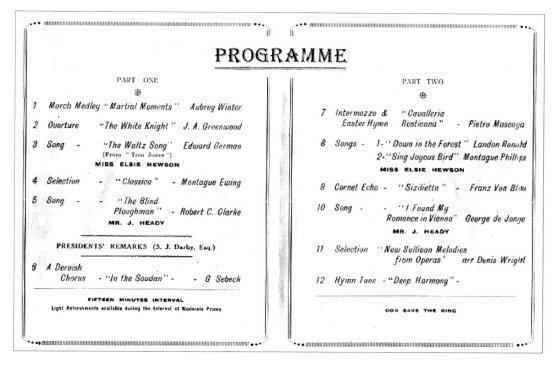

PROGRAMME

PART ONE

1   March Medley "Martial Moments"   Aubrey Winter

2   Overture   "The White Knight"   J. A. Greenwood

3   Song   -   "The Waltz Song"   Edward German
(From "Tom Jones")
MISS ELSIE HEWSON

4   Selection   -   "Classica"   -   Montague Ewing

5   Song   -   "The Blind Ploughman"   -   Robert C. Clarke
MR. J. HEADY

PRESIDENTS' REMARKS (S. J. Darby, Esq.)

6   A Dervish Chorus   -   "In the Soudan"   -   G. Sebeck

FIFTEEN MINUTES INTERVAL
Light Refreshments available during the Interval at Moderate Prices

PART TWO

7   Intermezzo &   "Cavalleria Rusticana"   -   Pietro Mascagna
Easter Hymn

8   Songs   -   1- "Down in the Forest"   Landon Ronald
2- "Sing Joyous Bird"   Montague Phillips
MISS ELSIE HEWSON

9   Cornet Echo   -   "Sizilietta"   -   Franz Von Blou

10   Song   -   "I Found My Romance in Vienna"   George de Jonge
MR. J. HEADY

11   Selection   "New Sullivan Melodies from Operas"   arr Denis Wright

12   Hymn Tune   -   "Deep Harmony"   -

GOD SAVE THE KING

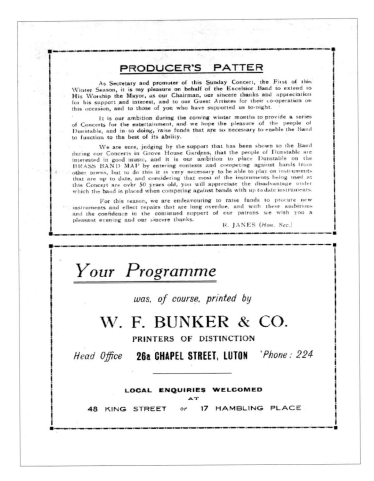

PRODUCER'S PATTER

As Secretary and promoter of this Sunday Concert, the First of this Winter Season, it is my pleasure on behalf of the Excelsior Band to extend to His Worship the Mayor, as our Chairman, our sincere thanks and appreciation for his support and interest, and to our Guest Artistes for their co-operation on this occasion, and to those of you who have supported us to-night.

It is our ambition during the coming winter months to provide a series of Concerts for the entertainment, and we hope the pleasure of the people of Dunstable, and in so doing, raise funds that are so necessary to enable the Band to function to the best of its ability.

We are sure, judging by the support that has been shown to the Band during our Concerts in Grove House Gardens, that the people of Dunstable are interested in good music, and it is our ambition to place Dunstable on the BRASS BAND MAP by entering contests and competing against bands from other towns, but to do this it is very necessary to be able to play on instruments that are up to date, and considering that most of the instruments being used at this Concert are over 50 years old, you will appreciate the disadvantage under which the band is placed when competing against bands with up to date instruments.

For this reason, we are endeavouring to raise funds to procure new instruments and effect repairs that are long overdue, and with these ambitions and the confidence in the continued support of our patrons we wish you a pleasant evening and our sincere thanks.

R. JANES (Hon. Sec.)

Your Programme

was, of course, printed by

W. F. BUNKER & CO.

PRINTERS OF DISTINCTION

Head Office   **26a CHAPEL STREET, LUTON**   '*Phone : 224*

LOCAL ENQUIRIES WELCOMED
AT
48 KING STREET   *or*   17 HAMBLING PLACE

The back page of the concert programme.

The Concert's Producer & Band Secretary – Mr. Dick Janes *(pictured opposite)*
His 'Producer's Patter' on the back page of the programme shows the importance attached to this opening concert in the series. The Band had acquired the services of the Mayor as Chairman of the Band. For some time it had been a tradition to ask or appoint the Mayor of Dunstable to the position of Chairman. (It is an interesting statement that 'most of the instruments were over 50 years old').

He also refers to their concerts in Grove House Gardens held on summer Sunday evenings when they played on the original bandstand, the circular rockery to the rear of the front lawns at the back of Grove House. Mr. Janes, whose first instrument was the E flat horn, had by 1949 become a long serving member of the Band, and also played with his brother in the Excelsior, (Fred Janes), in Fred's Dance Band – well known for their Town Hall dances. The advertisers, the Bunker family, had supported the Excelsior for some time, including collecting for Band funds on many occasions.

1940–1950 Period
The author's cousin, David Janes, whose father, Dick Janes, was secretary for seven years, recalls that era in a letter to the author, in March, 1998.

He had looked into his memorabilia cupboard and came up with the Town

Dick Janes is pictured above at his home in Dunstable in about 1949.

Hall programme for November 1949 (see illustrations).He could remember going to the old band room where practices were held, then they moved to another place which had quite a low ceiling and iron pillars supporting the roof – all a bit rusty – and which he thought was an old brewery building. There were a number of performances in Grove House Gardens in the summer, on Sunday evenings, and also concerts similar to the 1949 programme, with various guest artists. There were also dances in the Town Hall in aid of funds, using his uncle Fred Janes and his band (with Fred's son Roy in it as well – both members of the Excelsior). He imagined the Gazette would have reports of these (see second paragraph of 'Producers Patter'). The young David 'helped' at the dances by operating the spotlight from the balcony, or taking tickets at the door.

The 1949 group picture was probably taken soon after they bought new 'uniforms', (his Dad used to get a free ride on the bus when he wore his, especially if he stood on the platform). David also provided the single photo of him in his uniform, and holding his flugel horn, shown above. He thought the band room then was to the side of Priory House. He remembers there were a number of other music-making groups at about that time, such as 'Fred Boskett's Glee Club, and the Luton Girls Choir – also with singers from Dunstable who performed regularly at the Town Hall'.

The picture below shows a typical 'square' format practice layout as recalled by Jim Bull in the old building near Ashton St. which could have been the old abattoir.

1951 – CONCERT WITH THE DUNSTABLE GIRLS' CHOIR

A picture from the Dunstable Gazette taken in the summer of 1951.

An attentive audience is listening to the Dunstable Girls Choir, accompanied by the Excelsior Silver Prize Band, performing at the old (2nd) bandstand at the rear of Grove House Gardens in 1951. Fred Costin is at the piano. Florence Perry, the director of the Choir, can be seen to his left.

The bandstand was demolished in the nineteen-sixties, having had progressively less use and being in need of refurbishment by then. This does remind us however of early days when concerts were often held in Grove House Gardens, which still earlier took place on the circular rockery stand (the 'cake stand') typically on summer Sunday evenings. The original rockery site can still be found to the rear of the lawns at the back of Grove House.

Sunday Evening Concerts at AC-Delco

The photograph opposite shows the Band playing at one of a series of Sunday evening concerts held at the venue in the nineteen-fifties, 1952 in fact. The conductor is Mr. Jim Bull leading 22 or more of the Band, mainly comprising members of the 1949 line-up as illustrated in their Town Hall concert programme. This venue was a popular one in the 'fifties with many a Saturday night dance being held there, as well as other bookings. The building later gave way to a re-built and much improved factory and canteen-clubhouse, was then converted back to commercial use, but now in 2003 the firm has finally closed down.

A Gazette report of one such Sunday concert stated – 'An enjoyable concert was given by the Dunstable Excelsior Band in the AC-Delco clubroom on Sunday evening: *A euphonium solo, 'Rondo', by Mozart was given by Mr. G. Ashby, and items by the Band were – 'The Vanished Army', 'Estudiante', 'Swing of the Kilt', 'Negro Spirituals', 'March of the Bowmen', 'Shy Serenade', 'Famous Musical Plays', 'Nightfall in Camp', 'Amparita Roca', and the hymn tune 'Abide With Me'.*

THE EXCELSIOR AT THE AC-DELCO CLUBHOUSE (CANTEEN)

The Conductor, Mr. J. Bull thanked AC-Delco for the free use of the clubroom'. (The soloist, George Ashby was an accomplished brass musician who had come to this area from the famous Black Dyke Mills Band, in the 'thirties.

THE SILVER BATON PRESENTED TO JIM BULL 1952

'In Recognition of Sterling Service To The Excelsior Silver Prize Band Over Many Years'.

The photo above shows Mr. Jim Bull, conductor of the Excelsior, being presented with a silver decorated conductor's baton by the chairman of the Band's Trustees, Mr. S. J. Darby, at one of their Sunday evening concerts at the AC-Delco clubhouse in Dunstable. The year was probably again 1952. Jim still had the baton in pride of place at his home in Dunstable. A fairly recent photo in 2000 (overleaf) shows him holding the same baton.

A Portrait of Mr. Jim Bull of The Excelsior Band

The photos show Mr. Jim Bull in the year 2000 at his home in Dunstable where he lived with his wife Cathy, pictured, left, with the silver baton (see previous page) and right, with his trumpet with which until quite recently he sounded the 'Last Post' at the annual service of Remembrance at the war memorial in Priory Gardens.

He joined the Excelsior Silver Prize Band in the early 1930s and played in military bands & dance bands during the war. In addition to resuming with the Excelsior after the war, he played for many years with the Geoff Stokes Dance Band, as well as the Bible Class Orchestra, the Square, and many other musical combinations over the long period of his musical involvement in Dunstable & district.

Apart from his spell in wartime military bands, where he met & played with several well known people, he has never made his living in music – so much of his time being spent with the Excelsior Band, which has always relied on local musicians giving their own time to the cause.

He took over the conductor's baton of the Excelsior in the early 1950s and is to be seen in several of the photos featured in the book. Sadly he died in July 2002, but we are fortunate to have had his full participation in the project.

Practice Facilities

Over the many years of the Band's existence, the Band has moved from one site to another to maintain its practice capabilities, which required permanent facilities each time a new venue was needed. In its very early days when it was the Temperance movement that was the prime mover in the band's beginning and development, the founding patrons supplied all its needs from instruments & music to the rooms in which it rehearsed.

The leading Temperance citizens of the Town included the owners of the Commercial Hotel in West Street, the Marchant family. Other leading figures had a Hotel in High Street South. Other prominent citizens tended to be solid local businessmen & prominent in local non-conformism. There was therefore ample opportunity to provide rehearsal rooms where the band could not only play, but store the instruments provided for them, together with their music etc. It must also be remembered that several musicians played for other bands and orchestras (the Bible Class at the Square in particular) which could call upon their own facilities if required.

Mr. Jim Bull was the last but one of the conductors of the Excelsior, handing in his baton in 1958, (the last conductor being Fred Janes), and talked of the band for many years using the 'old abattoir' in St. Mary's Street, just along from the Wesleyan Institute near the Square, where they had permanent facilities laid out for them. In the centre of the main building was constructed a square 4-sided continuous music stand, open in the centre, similar to the earlier illustration. Around the walls were a series of hooks or hangers suitable for holding the band's instrument collection. The members would arrive, take their instruments down and deploy around the music square, according to the directions of the conductor of the period. The music parts would be distributed and rehearsals would begin. The instruments & music etc. were all owned by the Band as a whole and subject to the administration of the Patrons and the committee. Some members would own their own instruments (at home) but the bands own 'stock' so to speak had been purchased by the Patrons out of their own resources and the moneys raised from collections and fund raising events, so there was a full compliment of instruments available for newcomers, young trainees etc. Jim Bull recalls Sunday morning practice sessions which were highly disciplined affairs, although he speaks of one member of the renowned Dolman family hanging up his instrument at 12.30 sharp in order not to be late for his Sunday dinner, regardless of the circumstances of the practice e.g. in the middle of a tune, this was however always accepted in spite of any inconvenience!

The Last Move and The End of an Era

There of course came a time when the redevelopment of that area around St. Mary's Street required the demolition of the old abattoir, as well as most of that area which in many instances had become a slum. The Band then however was able to transfer to premises at Priory House – or more precisely to a wooden building within the grounds to the right of the entrance but which has since been replaced by public toilet facilities.

This took place about the mid to late 1950s, and it was during this period that the numbers began seriously to fall – television, competition from other areas (young people in particular found the commitment to a band regime difficult to accept in the new environment), all played their part in the decline, although Bands in other towns, e.g. Luton, and Heath and Reach among others have all managed to thrive up to and beyond the 2nd millennium. A musical friend & colleague of the author over many years, Mr. Paul Heley, was one of the last of the younger musicians to join the Band after leaving the RAF and wishing to continue his cornet playing. He recalls the hut used for practice at the time in 1955. He remembers being made very welcome and also being the only young musician in the band! Within a year, however, a meeting with some old school friends who were forming a jazz band (which was to become 'The Wayfarers'), led him to make the rather sad decision to leave the Excelsior – he recalls their good wishes to him nevertheless. He and those friends are still playing their jazz with others of the same era.

It was in 1960 that the members took the bold step of getting in touch with BBC TV, asking the 'Today' programme to put on a feature, with the band playing a selection of pieces and drawing attention to the band and its music, hoping that the publicity might lead to an improvement in their fortunes. The item was reported by one of the 'Today' team's leading presenters, Mr Derek Hart. Older 'viewers' may remember the actual programme. Mr.Hart was a regular reporter, with Cliff Michelmore as the main presenter. Sadly however this did not have the desired result, and not long afterwards the Excelsior Silver Prize Brass Band was wound up after 100 years of existence, and its assets disposed of. (The Old Borough Band had of course been wound up not long before the 2nd World War c.1938, after about 80 years or so of playing in the town).

So it was that when, in June of 1963, the Town Council & the Priory Church decided to produce the Pageant of Dunstable (qv), there was no band available in Dunstable to play for the production and the organisers had to look elsewhere, asking the excellent Heath & Reach Brass Band to do the honours.

Postscript

The Excelsior's period of existence saw many changes, locally and nationally, many of which conspired to cause the Band's demise. We are fortunate to have had the recollections and memorabilia of both veterans of the Dunstable music scene, and families and descendants of the Band, with whom the author also has connections.

Many hours of reminiscing have been spent with Jim Bull, who was the last but one conductor; Douglas Darby who was active in music in the town during the life of the Band – particularly with the Bible Class Orchestra (many members of the Excelsior also played with the Orchestra), Mrs. Mary Dolman, Mrs. Louie and Miss Jaquie Dolman, members of the Janes family and others. Douglas mentioned that the Excelsior used to play outside the homes of successful town councillors after local elections in the old Borough days – a situation rather unimaginable in modern times – reflecting the close connection of those local bands with the town in those days.

Amusing stories from Jim include one from the days before WWII when he and other members would play on a Saturday and finish up with a visit to a local hostelry or two, (obviously in the post-temperance era), when a particular colleague used to buy fish and chips for the policeman on duty at the cross-roads, taking them to him somewhat unsteadily in the middle of the road. On occasions when the PC was not present he would nevertheless walk to the middle of the road and place the fish and chips on the ground for when the officer returned.

Mrs. Louie Dolman has in her possession a very old ornate silver trombone dating back to the early Twentieth Century, in a leather case and wrapped in a trouser leg! The instrument had belonged to a member of the family who had died early in the century. It is ornately engraved and perhaps one day might be seen in a Dunstable museum. The Dolmans of course were strongly associated with the Excelsior, nine of the family playing at one time.

One or two attempts have been made over the years to re-form a town band, but without enduring success. It is hoped that this history will serve to remind Dunstablians of the times when the town and its celebrations were well served by its own 'community' bands. The Salvation Army of course still marches proudly on and the senior schools in the town carry on its musical traditions within the resources and scope of the education system, and all can be seen and heard from time to time at the Town Council's summer concerts in Grove House Gardens and elsewhere (see the following chapters), and the senior schools now regularly play on tours abroad.

7 THE SALVATION ARMY BAND

General History of the Salvation Army Bands

The first band to play for the Salvation Army was a somewhat modest group of two cornets, a valve trombone and a euphonium. It appeared in Salisbury, Wilts, in 1878, and its members were the Fry family, father Charles, and three sons (Fred, Ernest and Bert). Variously known as the *'Salisbury Brass Band'* and the *'Happy Band'* (also the *'Hallelulliah Minstrels'*), they were sometimes augmented to seven or eight instruments, adding another cornet, a baritone horn, a euphonium and a bass drum.

General Booth, the founder of the Salvation Army, after being informed of the group's abilities in calming extremely hostile crowds, came to see for himself, and was impressed enough to use them for a trial period, to accompany his own campaigns.

General Booth's statue in London.

In the meantime, two slightly larger ensembles appeared, one at Consett, Co. Durham, and another at Northwich, Cheshire. There was some dispute in later years about which was the earlier band and could thus claim the honour of being the first Corps. Band. The Durham Ensemble was eventually to be accorded that distinction, as it had been functioning towards the end of 1879, whereas the Northwich began their activities in 1880. An order was then issued in March 1880 directing Salvation Army officers and soldiers to learn to play instruments. Anyone who had an instrument lying idle was encouraged to send it to Headquarters. General Booth was not apparently fussy about musical balance, asking for violins, bass viols, concertinas, cornets or any brass instruments, drums, or anything else 'that will make a pleasant sound for the Lord.'

In a comparatively short space of time, however, Salvation Army bands developed into many small brass bands throughout the country, and in 1886 it was claimed that there were four hundred such groups in existence overall.

Not all of them may have been particularly skilled in those early days and local newspapers carried complaints from readers, or reports of disturbances, as the Army bands enthusiastically 'took to the streets for the Lord'! The activities of these bands were rarely mentioned in the brass band press, as the Salvation Army, unlike the Temperance movement, kept itself quite apart from the secular brass band world. They didn't enter contests, rarely played music other than their own, and in later years even played instruments manufactured by their own organisation (made in fact at their factory at St. Albans for many years).

However, in time, the Salvation Army bands developed into very good ensembles – enough to be respected by the most rigorous brass band

connoisseur, (George Bernard Shaw was a great admirer). In contrast to some hostility in earlier days, the Salvation Army and its bands became widely respected. The organisation's main influence on other brass bands, however, has mainly been through people who left their ranks and brought their talents as instrumentalists, conductors, composers or arrangers to the 'Civilian' bands.

The History of The Dunstable Salvation Army Band

The date of the inauguration of the Salvation Army in Dunstable is said to be the year 1886. The founding of the band may have been two years or more later however.

The location of their first citadel or meeting place in Dunstable is also to be established. We do know that in the nineteen-twenties premises in High Street North were used, namely the shop, later to be Green's the greengrocer and fruiterer featured in one of the following photographs. An undated press cutting refers to the Army holding their meetings '2 doors down from The Nag's Head'. The same item also stated that on special occasions they would meet at 'Tower House' in High Street North (which in the early part of the century was in 'Upper Houghton Regis'). This was the home of Alderman Mr. John Dales whose business manufactured 'Dales Dubbin', used for preserving leather and much used in the first World War on boots and saddles etc.

Mr. Dales was a town councillor for some years and was Mayor in 1919. His daughter Miss Lucy Dales was also active in the town and was Mayor in 1925. The Dales allowed their house to be used by other local organisations, in particular the Girl Guides, Miss Dales being closely associated with that movement.

The Army were welcome to use the hall at the house, and play in the grounds at the rear. Tower House was an impressive building in High Street North, with a 'pagoda' style upper storey opposite the entrance to Chiltern Road. It was demolished in the 1970s to make way for a petrol station, again demolished to become the site of a block of flats. (Next door to the left was another elegant house, home at one time of Admiral Sir Lionel Preston to whom the Sea Cadets HQ. at the Old Mill in West Street is dedicated, which house was also demolished at about the same time as Tower House).

The nineteen thirties saw the building of a purpose-built Citadel near the junction of Bull Pond Lane and St. Mary's Street. This building was to be superseded in the late 1990s by the present much larger premises fronting Bull Pond Lane, nearly opposite Bennett's Recreation ground. These new premises are also hired to other organisations as from the year 2000.

The Salvationists have had quite close links with the Methodist Church over the years. In 1944 Col. Mary Booth (daughter of the General) paid a visit to the Methodist Church in October of that year, and the event was featured in the local Press at that time.

Older Dunstablians will remember the Salvation Army Band marching and playing through the Town on Sunday mornings, often stopping at particular places where they would play for hymn singing with other Army members, not members of the Band, but including the 'Songsters' (mainly women members) who would add to the sound with tambourines to which were tied ribbons in the Army colours. The public were welcome to join in, and, if they wished, to contribute to a collection. The Band still follows that tradition of playing 'on the road' but in a format more suited to the demands of modern traffic etc.

The Band is particularly well known for playing at special occasions in the Town, for example the Remembrance Day Service, a multi denominational event. They also travel out of town and have played regularly at the Tree Cathedral in Whipsnade.

It is an interesting fact that not far away, in St. Albans, the Salvation Army used to have their own purpose built factory at which they manufactured their own instruments. A name that has been quoted in connection with St. Albans is Mr. Dennis Lofthouse 'who made tubas' at the factory. The St. Albans factory was finally closed down about fifteen years ago.

Another local name from the past is Mr. A. N. Philpott of Luton, who was a Salvationist himself but was also widely known locally amongst musicians of all denominations as a skilled repairer of brass instruments. He was able on one occasion to fully restore a cornet that had been squashed by a lorry! Earlier on Mr. Philpott had supplied and taken a full set of instruments to General Booth in London.

It is also a fact that the Army has for a long time printed and published their own music and indeed all Army publications, but about five or six years ago decided to release its music to outside bands. The Salvation Army has long been very self sufficient in its operations.

THE ST ALBANS FACTORY

Above, a photo of the Salvation Army's own instrument factory in St. Albans in 1904. Working conditions there were said to be much in advance of their time. The factory closed down many years ago. ('The British Bandsman')

This was one aspect of the original policy of self-sufficiency in the organisation in order to be able to properly control their facilities, including the publication of its own sheet music.

The following pages show a series of photographs of the band over a period of approx. 80 years. These have been provided from the collection of a member of the Band, Mr. Ray Jackson, whose father also played in the Dunstable Band for many years.

POSSIBLY THE EARLIEST PHOTO OF THE SALVATION ARMY BAND IN DUNSTABLE

The inclusion of this damaged photo here is simply on the grounds of age, interest, and rarity. It was taken from the upstairs window of a house ('Oaklands') in Chiltern Road nearly opposite Cross Street North, probably around 1912, (now demolished to make way for a block of flats). The houses on the corner are still recognisable today. The Band is deployed in the middle of the road in an age where little traffic would be likely to disturb them. The two young girls on the opposite corner are thought to be the author's mother and aunt at about the age of 6 to 8 years.

It has been suggested that it might be a 1st World War recruitment exercise, dated c.1914. However the figures to the mid-left of the picture seem unmistakeably to be lady songsters in Salvationist uniform.

THE ARMY BAND IN 1923

Back Row (L–R): George King, Tom Clarke, Alf Impey, Vic Sharp, Frank Bandy, Vic West, Arthur Buckingham, William Davis. Front Row (L–R): Levi Bandy, Arthur West, Sid Jackson, Ensign Flinton, Willis Cook, Lt. Collins, Alfred Starling, Fred West, Richard Streddar. Foreground: The two boys' surnames. (L–R): Sear and Bozier.

The above is an original of a postcard pictured in a Gazette press cutting dated as 1923. The musicians in the photo are as listed above.

This picture is again taken with a backdrop of trees etc, and may be the garden of Dr. Lathbury in West Street (as with many others at that time). Mr. Sid Jackson in the picture is the father of Ray Jackson who supplied the photograph. The copy has suffered some vertical 'banding' but is well worth including nevertheless.

The photo opposite above is another from the collection belonging to Mr. Ray Jackson. The photograph could have been taken at their premises in High St. North, which was later to be Messrs. Green's the greengrocers.

Some of the members have been identified as set out below the photo.

The date of the photograph opposite below is not certain, but has been estimated as 1932. It shows eleven young musicians with their tutors against a rural background, typical of the nineteen twenties – thirties. The backdrop could be Dr. Lathbury's garden in West Street or possibly the grounds of Tower House in High Street North, long since demolished, but as a large house owned by the Dale family with extensive gardens it was often the site of gatherings of local organisations and their photographs.

It is another from Mr. Ray Jackson's collection. Most of the names of those present are listed below the photo.

The Army has always encouraged young people to play, being of course the senior musicians of tomorrow.

THE DUNSTABLE SALVATION ARMY BAND ABOUT 1926

Back Row L–R, includes: Frank Bandy, Joe Bavister, ..., Levi Bandy. Mid Row L–R, includes: Stan Clarke, Les Clarke, George Clarke and Sid Jackson. Front Row L–R, includes: George Buckingham, with Willis Cook (Bandmaster), and George King.

THE SALVATION ARMY YOUTH BAND OF THE NINETEEN-THIRTIES

Back Row L–R: ...., Fred Bavister, Fred Henmans, ... Middle Row L–R: Jack Johnson, Len Gascoigne, ...(Officer), Chris Lloyd, ...(Officer), Les Clarke, ... Front Row L–R: Frank Dawes, Ivor Streddar.

1935 – KING GEORGE VI SILVER JUBILEE CELEBRATIONS

*The special service at the recreation ground, with the Salvation Army
and the Band in attendance.*

*The photo is from a de luxe version of the souvenir commemorative booklet of
the Jubilee, kindly lent by Mrs. C Mead.*

THE SALVATION ARMY BAND IN 1937 – CORONATION YEAR

(RJ)

Far Back Row L–R: George King, George Buckingham, Sam Bell.
Inner Back Row L–R: Frank Bandy, ..., Fred Bavister, Joe Bavister, ...
Next Row L–R: Chris Lloyd, Sid Jackson, Leslie Clark, ..., ..., Alf Impey, Dick Streddar, Stan Clarke,
Levi Bandy, ..., Herbert Stevens.
Front Row L–R: ....(Officer), Willis Cook, ...(Officer).

This photo, taken in 1937, Coronation year of George VI, shows members of the Dunstable Band, with other members of the Corps at the rear. The members are pictured in High Street North, outside their then premises, a former shop, decorated with bunting with their title displayed over the top of the shop frontage, later to become the premises of Messrs. Green.

THE SALVATION ARMY CITADEL – 1970

The Salvation Army Citadel pictured in 1970, at the junction of St. Mary's Street to the left (see the sign in picture), and Bull Pond Lane to the right.

The buildings were demolished in 1993 to make way for the new and much larger Citadel and social centre, now facing on to Bull Pond Lane. St. Mary's Street is now defunct, forming part of the car park and access areas between the Salvation Army Citadel, the Ashton Square precinct, and the Wesleyan Church.

The entrance road to the car park & surrounding area from West Street, however, still perpetuates the name 'St. Mary's Street' in being named 'St. Mary's Gate'.

Opposite below: Although 1886 has been given earlier as the inaugural year for the Dunstable Corps, the celebration in 1985 of their Centenary Year indicates that the official setting up of a Dunstable Corps was registered in 1885, but may not have got under way until the following year. The illustrations show both sides of the Celebratory leaflet with the order of events shown on the right. The Centenary launch weekend was scheduled for the 8th & 9th of June. A 'Field Day' is listed for the 7th September.

October 23rd was set aside for the International Staff Songsters to appear. Although the Dunstable Band is not referred to as such, we can be sure they were very active throughout the whole year's celebrations.

14TH & 15TH MAY, 1983 CONCERT AT THE PRIORY CHURCH

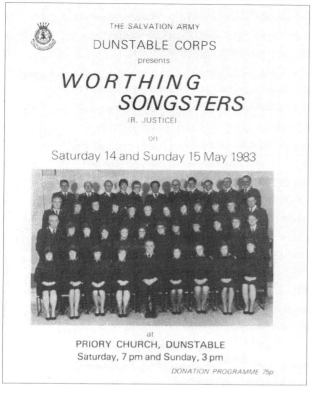

THE SALVATION ARMY

DUNSTABLE CORPS

presents

WORTHING
SONGSTERS

(R. JUSTICE)

on

Saturday 14 and Sunday 15 May 1983

at

PRIORY CHURCH, DUNSTABLE

Saturday, 7 pm and Sunday, 3 pm

DONATION PROGRAMME 75p

Left is the front page of the Programme of events for the 14th–15th May, 1983. Two concerts were performed, featuring the Worthing Songsters, backed by the Dunstable Corps Band. Both events were held in the Priory Church in Dunstable and were open to all denominations, and the general public to attend. Two of the Songsters in the photograph were formerly from the Dunstable Corps.

CENTENARY PROGRAMME FOR THE YEAR 1985

THE SALVATION ARMY
DUNSTABLE CORPS

Centenary Year 1985

SOUVENIR FOLDER

Diary of Events

Sun. 6th Jan.	-	Day of Renewal
Wed. 16th Jan.	-	Talk, "The Spirit of the Old Army" by General F. Coutts (R)
Wed. 20th Feb.	-	House Meeting
Wed. 20th Mar.	-	House Meeting
Wed. 17th Apr.	-	House Meeting
Wed 15th May	-	House Meeting
June 8th & 9th		Centenary Launching Weekend with the British Commissioner (Comm. & Mrs. Francy Cachelin)
June 29th & 30th	-	Young People's Anniversary Weekend : Major Mrs. Audrey Neal
Sat. 7th Sept.	-	Field Day
Sept. 28th & 29th	-	Harvest Weekend : Major & Mrs. F. Newnes
Oct. 21st - 25th	-	Various events for the Young People's Corps (Half-term week)
Wed. 23rd Oct.	-	International Staff Songsters
Tues. 12th Nov.	-	Bible Study
Thurs. 14th Nov.	-	Bible Study
Nov. 16th & 17th	-	Weekend Meetings led by Commissioner and Mrs. Will Cairns
Friday 29th Nov. to Sun. 1st Dec	-	Final Celebrations : Colonel & Mrs. John Dale

Here we see the Dunstable Salvationists' Youth Band pictured in the mid to late 1980s. On the right is Mr. Ray Jackson who had been looking after the young musicians for some time. They are photographed outside the old Citadel in Bull Pond Lane.

THE DUNSTABLE ARMY'S YOUTH BAND IN THE 1980s

(RJ)

This photograph can be compared to the youth band of c.1932 pictured earlier.

ON THE ROAD IN THE 1980s

Members above include Chris Edmonds, Joan Papps, Robert & Marian Noble and Tommy Spratt, probably in 1980, playing in a leafy avenue. The Band still goes on the road, but not so often through the middle of the town as in earlier years, unless for a special occasion as below, en route for the 'Queensway'.

REMEMBRANCE DAY 1987

The Salvation Army Band heads the Remembrance Day procession to the War Memorial in Priory Gardens in November 1987, (below). The Band makes its vital contribution every year to the Memorial services. The Last Post was sounded by Mr. Jim Bull (left) who at 71 years of age well remembered his own days in the 2nd World War. He performed this duty for many years.

Mr. Bull played & conducted in the former Dunstable Excelsior Brass Band for many years.

(DG)

PRIORY GARDENS APRIL 1988

For many years, the Town Council with the District Council & Vauxhall Motors, sponsored a summer programme of Concerts in Priory Gardens.

The concerts were always popular and the backdrop of the Priory Church, with the gardens, added to the experience. There were restrictions on the facilities able to be put in place in the Gardens, but the public did not appear to let it spoil their enjoyment.

Here in 1988 the Army concert is also supported by 'Octave' music. From the millennium year 2000, the venue changed to the new performance area in Grove House Gardens and the tradition continues in its new home.

THE SALVATION ARMY BAND IN GROVE HOUSE GARDENS, SUMMER 2001

8 THE KENSWORTH BRASS AND SILVER BAND

The existence of a band in the inter-war years in the village of Kensworth was originally brought to the author's notice by a friend and musical colleague, Mr. Trevor Evans. He was born and brought up in the village, and, although the band had ceased to exist before he was born, his family had had relatives in the band. He produced a cutting from the Dunstable Gazette in 1973 showing a group photo of the band taken in about 1923. Full details of the personnel were included, and the source of the photo, Mrs.Betty Tarbox of Dunstable, (her father played drums in the band). Betty provided the original photo below, and the names of all the musicians.

THE BAND IN 1923

Back Row L–R: F. Flitton, S. Dumpleton, A. King, A. King, A. Copcott, L. Whinnett, H. Busby, B. Isles, S. Willis, F. Tomlin (with the bass drum). Middle Row L–R: G. Hughes, L. Hughes, S. Ellins, R. Tomlin, D. Bell, G. Skinner, E. Evans, S. Harris, T. Ward. Front Row L–R: A. Flitton, G. Hill, H. Ward, S. Taylor, D. Willis, C. Whinnett, F. Ward.

Trevor and Betty put the author in touch with two people with vital connections with the band. The first, a surviving member of the band, was Trevor's uncle, Mr. Howard Ward, (3rd left, front row), who lived in Dunstable for many years, and at the ripe old age of 92, had been able to clearly recollect his time in the band.

The second, the son of another original member, and still living in Kensworth, was Mr. Fred Willis, whose father Mr. S. Willis played the Eb Horn in the band. Trevor was able to contact his other surviving uncle Mr. Ashley Ward who lives in Borough Road Dunstable, a few doors from Howard. Ashley who is also in his 90s, was not in the band, but nevertheless recognised all the musicians in the photograph of 1923 as they are listed below the picture. Betty Tarbox's father, Mr. Fred. Tomlin, was well known as a local coal merchant, and he became the band's drummer following the departure of the original drummer, Mr. J. Batchelor.

REMEMBRANCE DAY AT KENSWORTH CHAPEL MEMORIAL 1919

The memorial has since been re-positioned following demolition of older buildings etc.

Fred Willis has provided two interesting additional photographs of the band, the one above portraying the band at the Remembrance Day service in Kensworth, probably in 1919, and another below, also a Remembrance Day event, actually in Studham, at the inauguration of the Memorial Clock on the Common.

REMEMBRANCE DAY AT STUDHAM 1920

The Band at the dedication of the Memorial Clock.

The Band becomes The 'Silver' Band

Both Howard & Fred recall that the band was formed in 1919, not long after the First World War had ended. It was founded by Mr.(Francis Domino) Bowles, who is said to have been the chairman of the Pearl Assurance Company and lived at 'Bleak Hall' in the village from 1914 to 1924. He it was who bought all the instruments, trained the players, and provided a striking set of uniforms as pictured below. He and others in Kensworth thought it would be a healthy interest for the men of the village after the trauma of the 'Great' war.

Howard remembers marching through Luton from Park Square to the Wardown Memorial Park where they set up on the bandstand and played to the audience assembled there. On another occasion they travelled as far afield as London and played for a Pearl Assurance Company dinner, doubtless due to the patronage of Mr. Bowles. The band also frequently used to play at the foot of Dunstable Downs in West Street. As far as band practice was concerned, this was mainly carried out at the Chapel Sunday School in the village, where they also practised marching. They also regularly played in a room at the rear of the Women's Institute building at the edge of the recreation ground.

(IM)

Forward to the 'thirties. The village shop was the backdrop for the photo above, showing the very smart uniform of members of the 'Silver Band' as they had come to be known – but the date when the uniforms were acquired is not yet known.

Howard also recalls practising on occasions at the 'White Horse' in Church Street in Dunstable. In fact the landlord at the 'White Horse' at the time was Septimus Franklin of the well-known Franklin family – stalwarts of the Dunstable Brass Band, who also not surprisingly played there as well! (they have their own story in a separate chapter).

Another of Howard's recollections was that of taking part in a Band Contest which was held at Toddington. Among the other competitors were the Luton Band and the Earls Barton Band. He doesn't remember actually winning, but it must have been a big step for the band to enter a Contest, although possibly the only occasion. From time to time a player might guest with another local band and vice versa. Howard mentioned Messrs. Bonham, Owens, and (Charlie) Mantle joining with the Kensworth band at times, and also Fred Tomlin playing (drums) with the Luton Band alongside the famous Harry Mortimer.

The band's prime mover, Mr. Bowles, was also connected to the 'Diamond' factory in Luton (The Davis Gas Stove Co.), where Howard and several others worked. Howard had moved to Dunstable in fact when he married, living in Borough Road where he and his wife started their married life.

The Jubilee of King George V & Queen Mary in May 1935

This event was widely celebrated in the district and Kensworth's celebrations were reported in the Luton News & Beds. Advertiser. The paper told its readers that the day began a comprehensive programme with a united service at the recreation ground. The hymn singing was led by the Silver Band, and the accompanist for the psalms was Miss Mildred Dumpleton. The fancy dress parade was 'the finest ever seen in the village'. Tea was provided for nearly four hundred. About fifty ex-servicemen were entertained to supper by the Vicar & toasted by Mr. S. Willis supported by Mr. Tomlin and Mr. Tanner. The day ended with a firework display under the direction of Mr. Tanner & Mr. Geering and a huge bonfire under the charge of Mr. W. Fossey.

There are familiar names and associations in connection with the Band in the report, and this helps to identify the photograph above featuring the Moulster family in fancy dress and the Bandsmen in the background as being taken at the Jubilee fete, with the lower picture showing the Silver Band as a group, photographed in the recreation ground with the 'sports' sign at the back.

Another photo has come to light showing a section of a small group of players of a more senior age, from Mrs. Millest's collection, but the date of which is uncertain. It could be either just before or just after World War II and could have been an attempt to get a band together from veterans still living in the village.

THE LATEST PICTURE

Six players appear to be partly within the original picture but the three middle musicians can be clearly seen. The player on the left has been identified as Mr. Edwin Evans. The photo originated from Home Counties Newspapers, and could have been featured in the 'Gazette' at the time.

Postscript

Howard and Betty also spoke of 'Uncle Rupert' conducting the band from time to time both generally, and more specifically at the 'Diamond' factory – on the untimely death of Mr. Bowles in 1925. The passing of Mr. Bowles had a devastating effect on the band, which was not surprising when his enormous support, and sponsorship of the band is remembered. In fact it appears that the band may have continued only until the late thirties after it had lost the momentum provided by Mr. Bowles. However, in spite of its relatively short lifespan, a large body of musicians made up a thriving brass band in Kensworth for a number of years between the wars, and it is well worth telling its story. Finally Howard remembers the instruments being sold and the proceeds donated to the church choir and others in the village.

HOWARD WARD

Howard Ward, June 2000, in his garden in Dunstable. (Sadly he died in 2001 at 94.)

9 THE HEATH BAND

THE HEATH (& REACH) BRASS BAND 1935

(MD

The picture above, published as a 'bygone' in the local press, was supplied by Mr. John Saint of Leighton Buzzard (5th from left, centre row). It was taken in 1935. Also identified is the drummer Mr Ron Lansbury. The Band's history goes back to the year 1933, when a group of six friends decided to form a Brass Band. The picture below was taken in the early 1940s outside the village barn in Heath and Reach which served as their headquarters for many years.

THE HEATH BAND IN THE 1940s

(PF)

A PRE-1954 PHOTO IN FRONT OF THE VILLAGE BARN

(PF)

This photograph is thought to date back to 1952, a year or two before the Secretary, Peter Farmer's father joined the Band. There are 26 persons in the picture, the same number as the Band in 2003! The 'Village Barn', not the 'Village Hall', is the name of the building that has served the Band for many years. The two persons mid-centre are holding a cup and base, indicating the photo may well have been called to commemorate the Band's most recent success at the time, in the Contest field.

THE BAND IN THE VILLAGE BARN IN THE 1960s

(PF)

The Band is posing for a set piece photo, proudly displaying a selection of their Contest trophies.

The Heath Band is one of an increasing number of bands to have set up its own web site, setting out a brief history of the band, with a series of photographs, and a list of forthcoming programmes and events. These views of the band on stage and 'in the field' were taken from their web site as at February 2002. The site also permits the viewer to hear the Band playing four tunes from its repertoire, if the computer is suitably equipped.

PICTURES FROM THE 2002 WEBSITE

Left, the Band is pictured on an exchange tour, playing 'al fresco' at Coulommiers in France, (Leighton Buzzard's twin town). The Heath Band has a link with that town's Accordion Band, and regular exchanges take place between the two.

The Heath Band has also played in other places in France, including Fontainebleu, Chantilly, Paris and Versailles.

THE HEATH BAND AT THE CEDARS SCHOOL 1999

PLAYING AT THE SHUTTLEWORTH AIR MUSEUM IN 2000

(PF)

THE HEATH BAND IN CONCERT IN 2000

(PF)

The Band is pictured playing at a Concert in the year 2000, at the Baptist Chapel, Leighton Buzzard.

THE HEATH BAND 'AT HOME' IN 2001

(PF)

The Heath Band, resplendent in their uniforms, pose in the Village in 2001.Seated front row centre is the Band's conductor, Mr. David Phillips.

The Heath Band currently has twenty-six members in the Senior Band, and a thriving Junior Band of sixteen or so members from the age of seven upwards. At present, they have decided to suspend their Contest activities, but have recently recorded a live session of the Band at the Cedars School in Leighton Buzzard, and it is hoped that a CD will be issued in due course. This reminded us that the Band recorded some music for the Dunstable Pageant in 1963, some forty years ago, and listening to the recording recently (on a mini-disc transcription by the author), came as a pleasant surprise to the present Secretary. Further details can be found in the later chapter on the Pageant.

These recent photographs have been kindly supplied by the Secretary of the Heath Band, Mr. Peter Farmer, several of whose family are either members of the Band or connected with the Brass Band world. Mr. Brian Rolls is the Bandmaster, and the Conductor is Mr. David Phillips. (Peter's father, John, is conductor of the Toddington Town Band).

10 THE GREAT BRICKHILL BAND

THE GREAT BRICKHILL BRASS BAND

(SB)

The musicians named in the photo are:
Back Row L–R: Charlie Dickens, Will Dickens, Mr. Yates.
Front Row L–R: Tom Dickens, Joe Hall, A. Hobbs, Archie Moss, Fred Battoms.

The band is seated in front of a door draped with a tricolour banner on which it appears to say 'Peace and Plenty'. Another similar banner is draped to the right.

It would seem that a special occasion is being celebrated – with most members sporting buttonholes. A 'Lyons Tea' sign can also be seen to the top right of the photo, and in the bottom middle of the window is probably a menu. The building is thought to have been the former 'Spinning Wheel' Café in the village, demolished many years ago.

THE BAND PICTURED WITH OTHERS TAKING PART IN THE CELEBRATIONS

(SB)

This photograph puts the earlier example in a fuller context. The members of the Band are all present within this larger group and the wider view appears to confirm the venue as the 'Spinning Wheel'.

How long the band existed, and when it was founded are so far not known. If the photo was taken before the 1st World War, some of those pictured may not have returned, and it is a little odd that the Union Jack is not shown. Some local bands were set up after the end of the war, which would make the date around 1919. 'Peace & Plenty' could represent a hope for the future.

The occasion however is still uncertain. The tricolour flags must be central to the event which was obviously a village celebration, buttonholes much in evidence, and everyone in their best outfits. The coronation of Edward VII has been suggested, but that would place the date at 1903.

The group includes a gentleman with a collection box to the right, with to his right the current custodian of the jug of ale, and possibly 'mine host' in the centre in the shirt sleeves. We are informed that the animal front left was a 'singing dog'! The young people sitting at the front include the only females in the picture, which comprises thirty-one persons overall. A curious feature is an apparently 'headless' man behind the jug of ale – he is nevertheless included in the head count.

11 THE TODDINGTON TOWN BAND

A Brief History

Evidence of the existence of brass band music in Toddington goes back a long way, in fact to the middle of the 19th century where the earliest documented reference so far found is recorded in the *Dunstable Chronicle* in 1856, which in its reports of the Peace celebrations in that year told its readers that The Toddington Brass Band played in the village with a group of family entertainers called the 'Morfey Family'(a well known group of entertainers in the North London area in those days).

This was a time when local papers were springing up all over the country after the Government finally removed the repressive stamp duty on newsprint. It is quite possible therefore in Toddington, Dunstable and elsewhere that groups of brass players could have been formed some years earlier than 1856 – see the chapter on the development of brass bands. Three years later, the *Chronicle* reported that on the 16th June 1859 in Toddington – 'The Oddfellows Annual Festival' was held at the 'Sow and Pigs', when a large procession of personnel in full regalia was headed by the 'Toddington Brass Band'.

The *Chronicle* ceased publication in 1860, and it wasn't until 1865 that the *Dunstable Borough Gazette* started publication. Occasional Press references may be found in later years, although there is nothing to suggest an unbroken link to the founding of the 'Toddington Town Band' in the early years of the 20th Century, when in 1910 the first conductor of the new Town Band was Mr.James Hyde.

James Hyde wielded the baton until his death in 1951. During that time the band had several successes in the Contest field, with successes in 1937 at Reading, and again in 1947 where they came 2nd in the Area Contest. This was followed by a 3rd place at the prestigious Belle Vue Contest in Manchester, gaining 3rd place in the 4th section. On James' death, his son Denis took over the conductor's chair; he also played trumpet and cornet. He combined this role with that of musical director of the Vauxhall Orchestra and Ladies' Choir.

Denis led the Band until his untimely death in 1982. At this point the Band came to a temporary halt. However in 1987, Denis's widow Beryl approached local brass teacher, Mr. Kevin Nicholls, to see if he would be interested in reviving the Band. He called a meeting of local players and was able to restart the Band, and it has since gone from strength to strength. In 2003, the Band now has thirty or so members including several young people and has its own web site, which sets out forthcoming programmes of events and is well worth a visit.

The following archive photographs were kindly provided by Mrs. Beryl Hyde who played in the Band (under her maiden name, Beryl Evans).

THE TODDINGTON BAND IN 1916

Above: This is so far the earliest known photograph of the Band, taken in 1916. It is not certain as to the site, or the names of all those present of whom there are nineteen in number. However, reference to the photo taken in 1920 may help to identify some of the bandsmen. It can be seen on the bass drum that at that time the Band was known as the 'Toddington Brass Band', but of course later on, and nowadays, it is called 'The Toddington Town Band'.

Opposite above: It is still to be established as to where the picture opposite above was taken. Beryl Hyde thinks it may possibly be at a farm in what was then called 'Gas Street', later called Conger Lane. With references to 'Oddfellows' it may have been taken at the rear of or near to the 'Oddfellows Arms', which may have been the origin of references to that name in the 19th century, as an alternative to the Oddfellows Friendly Society reference. Perhaps the two are linked.

Opposite below: The photo was taken in the year 1928, with the band proudly wearing its first uniform. Two years earlier, in 1926, they had appeared at a Contest at the Crystal Palace with James Hyde on solo cornet, (also playing with the Luton Red Cross Band at this time). There are twenty-two uniformed players in the group, with eight others present – including the Rev. Hunt centre-front. The venue of the photograph is still to be identified. It is likely that many of those named in previous pictures will still be present, but of course now they all have uniforms, complete with caps, it may be a little more difficult to identify all their names. However Beryl Hyde has identified several of those present.

THE TODDINGTON TOWN BAND IN 1920 – JAMES HYDE, CONDUCTOR

Some of the names of those in the above photo taken in 1920 were listed on an attachment to the photograph, and are as shown below.

Top Row L–R: 'Doings'(a local nickname), Mr. Pateman, Josh Denton, Ernie Buckingham (from Oddfellows), Reg. Buckingham, Mr. Hurst.

Middle Row L–R: Jock Ayres, Billy Brazier, Bob Ansell, Jack Hyde, Billy Webb.

Bottom Row L–R: Tom Whitbread, Mr. Hucklesby, Mr. Ansell, Aunt Kit (from Oddfellows), Jimmy Hyde, lady unknown, Horace Brown, Gordon.............

1928 – THE BAND WITH ITS FIRST UNIFORMS

Some of those present include: Stan Roberts, Trombone; Mr. George, Trombone; Arthur Seymour, Horn; Bob Ansell, Baritone Horn; Bill Joy, Cornet; Laurie Muckleston, Cornet; James Hyde, Cornet; Sam Browne, B flat Bass; Alfie Garner, Euphonium; The Rev. Hunt.

1935

Above, 1935 and brand new uniforms are the order of the day at this function held at Tingrith Manor. The band played for dancing in the evening.

Below, 1936, the Toddington Town band leads a parade of Old Contemptibles Association members from the Moor to the Parish Church in Luton on July 10th.

1936

Pictured in a local paper, the cutting dated 11.7.1936.

THE READING CONTEST 1937 – 2 TROPHIES WERE WON

(HCN)

It was their 5th and biggest success during the year. The conductor Mr. J. B. Hyde is seated centre, with Mrs. R. Fawcett to his right; Denis Hyde front, 2nd right.

THE TODDINGTON TOWN BAND IN 1942

This time the Band is pictured marching and playing for the Home Guard Parade in the year 1942; there was still sufficient a number in this 3rd year of World War II to keep the Band going, in fact during WWII the band was called the 'Home Guard Band'. It can be seen that the Band comprises mainly younger people, with James Hyde leading the marchers and proudly displaying his medals, including the WWI Belgian Croix de Guerre. To the middle right of the photo can be seen Beryl Hyde (Evans at the time) and another young lady called Rita Bunning (back left).

The marchers can be seen passing buildings still familiar in the Town, to the right, George Hart's the Newsagents, and on the left, Messrs. Barbers bakery, with the first two letters of the Hovis sign visible in the picture.

THE BAND IS PICTURED 'AT HOME', AFTER PLAYING AT THE BRIGHTON CONTEST IN 1947

The Band won the 'Plummer Hoddis' Cup which was presented by the Brighton Summer Queen, who had come up from Brighton for the occasion, (seen seated on the lower right). Also in the photograph is the Rev. Hunt, left, with Mr. Ainsworth and Mr. Jack Ladds.

Below, the band is seen relaxing under the trees at Brighton.

THE PRESENTATION OF THE 1947 TROPHY

Beryl Evans (later Hyde) proudly receives the 'Plummer Hoddis' Cup from the visiting Brighton Summer Queen *on behalf of the Toddington Town Band. Denis Hyde was also featured on solo cornet. This photo is particularly treasured by Beryl as on the reverse is this personal message from no less than the legendary Harry Mortimer – 'To Beryl, with the wish – May your lip never crack – Harry Mortimer'.*

THE 1952 READING FESTIVAL CONTEST PROGRAMME

MILITARY BAND SECTION.

(28 Performers)

PLUS TWO DRUMS

IN OLYMPIA, LONDON STREET.   DRAW at 3-30 p.m.

Adjudicator: Mr. A. V. Creasey.

TEST PIECE: " Egmont " Overture __ *Beethoven.*

PRIZES

First, Cash £15:15:0 and the " Frank W. Neale " Challenge Bowl.
Second, Cash £12:12:0.
Third, Music to the value of £2:2:0, kindly presented by Messrs. Boosey & Hawkes.

Band.	Conductor.	Playing No.	Result.
1. CHISWICK MEM. CLUB	Mr. N. Bowden		
2. EPSOM B.L.	Mr. N. Bettinson		
3. LYMINGTON BOROUGH	Mr. F. J. S. Loveday		
4. READING MILITARY	Mr. C. Godfrey		
5. TOTTENHAM MILITARY	Mr. C. R. Gardner, M.B.E.		

VISIT THE

EXHIBITION of . . .
BAND EQUIPMENT

in the Crush Lobby and Small Town Hall

BY LEADING FIRMS IN THE BAND WORLD

THE ARMY AND NAVY SUPPLY STORES, LTD.
Designers and Makers of Uniforms.
Messrs. BESSON & CO. LTD.
Messrs. BOOSEY & HAWKES LTD.
Messrs. HOPE BROTHERS.
Messrs. MAYERS & HARRISON.
Messrs. R. SMITH & CO.
Messrs. THE UNIFORM CLOTHING & EQUIPMENT CO. LTD.
Messrs. BRISTOL BAND INSTRUMENT CO. (at Olympia).

The National Brass Band Club will be represented by
Mr. E. Griggs and Mr. T. Morcombe.
The National Association of Brass Band Conductors will be represented by
Mr. S. A. Early.

Parnells the Printers Ltd., Reading

BERKSHIRE & NEIGHBOURING COUNTIES

BAND FESTIVAL GUILD

*Promoted by the " Reading Mercury " and " Berkshire Chronicle "
Newspapers.*

President:

H. A. BENYON, Esq. (Lord Lieutenant of Berkshire).

Vice-President : C. M. HOBSON, Esq., M.A.

Mr. H. Mortimer, O.B.E., Adjudicator and Conductor.

Sixteenth Annual Festival

With the co-operation of Neighbouring Associations.

TOWN HALLS and OLYMPIA, READING

SATURDAY, NOVEMBER 8th, 1952

Programme, 6d.

*Above: The front and back covers of the programme, autographed by Harry Mortimer, the adjudicator.
Below: The programme's inner pages.*

SECTION III. BRASS or BRASS and REED.

(20 Performers).

IN THE LARGE TOWN HALL, at 1-30 p.m.   DRAW at 1 p.m.

Adjudicator : Mr. E. Dadson.

TEST PIECE : Fantasia, " Country Life " __ *F. Le Duc.*

PRIZES

First, Cash £8:8:0 and the National Brass Band Silver Challenge Cup.
Second, Cash £5:5:0 and the Boosey & Hawkes Challenge Shield.
Third, Cash £3:3:0.
A Special Prize, Music to the value of £2:2:0, kindly presented by Messrs. Beeson & Co.,
will be awarded to the smallest competing band, placed highest apart from the
first three.

Band.	Conductor.	Playing No.	Result.
1. ALDERSHOT TOWN	Mr. G. Prior		
2. BASINGSTOKE SILVER	Mr. A. Russell		
3. BEENHAM BRASS	Mr. A. Garrett		
4. CHINNOR SILVER	Mr. D. W. Lewis		
5. CHOLSEY PRIZE	Mr. G. Watkins		
6. EAST WOODHAY SILVER	Mr. D. Webb		
7. HENLEY TOWN	Mr. F. Edwards		
8. HIGHWORTH TOWN	Mr. S. B. Harman		
9. HOOK, ODIHAM & DISTRICT	Mr. W. Williams		
10. HORSHAM BRITISH LEGION	Mr. G. Arnell		
11. POTTERS BAR TOWN	Mr. A. T. Cheek		
12. SANDHURST SILVER	Mr. Hughes		
13. THATCHAM SILVER	Mr. G. Watkins		
14. TODDINGTON JUNIOR	Mr. D. W. Hyde		

SECTION I. BRASS.

(25 Performers).

IN THE LARGE TOWN HALL, at 3 p.m. (approx.).   DRAW at 2-30 p.m.

Adjudicator: Mr. H. Mortimer, O.B.E.

TEST PIECE : Suite " Spring Time " __ *Haydn Morris.*

PRIZES

First, Cash £15:15:0 and the " William Vincent " Silver Challenge Cup.
Second, Cash £12:12:0 and the " Besson " Challenge Shield.
Third, 3 Handsome Music Stands, kindly presented by The Uniform Clothing and
Equipment Co., Ltd.

Band.	Conductor.	Playing No.	Result.
1. AVELEY SILVER	Mr. L. R. J. Nicholls		
2. BOSCOMBE SILVER	Mr. C. J. Young		
3. BOXMOOR SILVER	Mr. R. Hutchinson		
4. JOHN DICKINSONS (Apsley)	Mr. P. B. Catelinet		

CHAMPIONSHIP SECTION BRASS

(25 Performers).

IN THE LARGE TOWN HALL, at 3 p.m.   DRAW at 3 p.m.

Play commences at termination of Section I.

Adjudicator : Mr. H. Mortimer, O.B.E.

TEST PIECE : " Festival Overture " __ *H. Geehl.*

PRIZES

First, Cash £25:0:0 and the " Reading Mercury " Silver Challenge Vase.
Second, Cash £15:15:0 and the " Mayers & Harrison " Cup.
Third, Cash £10:10:0.

Band.	Conductor.	Playing No.	Result.
1. FURNITURE INDUSTRIES	Dr. Denis Wright		
2. HAZELLS (Aylesbury)	Mr. J. Alderson		
3. JOHN DICKINSONS (Apsley)	Mr. P. B. Catelinet		
4. LEWIS MERTHYR (Porth)	Mr. O. D. Jones		
5. PRESSED STEEL CO.	Mr. H. W. Roberts, A.R.C.M.		
6. RAUNDS TEMPERANCE	Mr. O. Pentelow		

SECTION II. BRASS.

(24 Performers).

IN OLYMPIA, LONDON STREET, at 2 p.m.   DRAW at 1.30 p.m.

Adjudicator: Mr. A. V. Creasey.

TEST PIECE : " Three Songs Without Words " __ *Eric Ball.*

PRIZES

First, Cash £10:10:0 and the " Berkshire Chronicle " Silver Challenge Cup.
Second, Cash £6:6:0 and the " Guild " Challenge Shield.
Third, Cash £4:4:0.
Fourth, Music value £2:2:0, presented by R. Smith & Co.

Band.	Conductor.	Playing No.	Result.
1. BERKHAMSTED ST. PETERS	Mr. W. F. Williams		
2. BURLEY SILVER	Mr. S. E. Crutcher		
3. CHIPPING NORTON SILVER	Mr. W. H. Pickett		
4. EGHAM & DISTRICT	Mr. A. Clay		
5. HASLEMERE	Mr. J. B. Thomas		
6. HEATH EXCELSIOR	Mr. T. Boyes		
7. KENNET VALE	Mr. F. G. Lewis		
8. PARKEND SILVER	Mr.		
9. SOUTH STREET MIS.	Mr. J. E. Garratt		
10. ST. SEBASTIAN'S PARISH	Mr. E. F. Repper		
11. TOWCESTER STUDIO	Mr. W. J. Bell		
12. WEST CHILTINGTON S.	Mr. A. Slater		

CHRISTMAS 1960

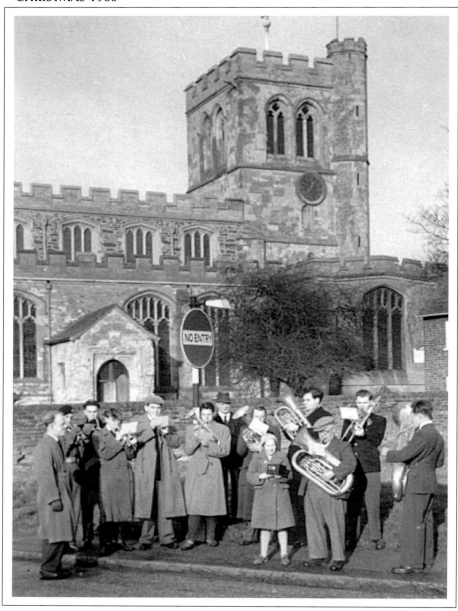

(BH

It is Christmas 1960, and members of the Toddington Town Band play outside the Church on what appears to be a fine winter's day – the time on the church clock stands at 12.40 p.m. No uniforms in evidence here, but it is obviously warm enough for some of the players to dispense with their overcoats.

The photograph opposite appears to be one of the last photos of the Band so far available before the Band was temporarily wound up for a period, until it was revived in 1987.

THE JUNIORS IN 1961

Toddington Juniors at Tanners End Church Fete in 1961. This photo from Beryl Hyde shows a section of the band's junior players. (Photo Carol Gibbs – Tingrith – per BH)

1963 AND 1964 MUSIC FESTIVALS

The certificates speak for themselves – dated March 1963 and 1964 respectively (approx. quarter size).

THE TODDINGTON TOWN BAND IN THE PARK AT DUNSTABLE 2001

(AW

A picture of the Band, taken by digicam, playing at the Performance Area in Grove House Gardens, Dunstable. The Band is being watched by a large and appreciative crowd on a sunny Sunday afternoon in July 2001.

The New Millennium

Today, following the Jubilee year 2002, the Band has thirty or so members, including many young people, who are taking the Toddington Town Band into the new millennium in fine form, under their musical director, Mr. John Farmer. Their Bandmaster is Mr. Ian M. Smith, with Secretary Derek Jones, Treasurer Danny Nemar, and Social Secretary David Beal.

The Band's modern image in this computer age can be gauged by their Internet web site which provides updated information on the Band with their programme of future Concerts. Readers can access their web site on (http://www.ttb.org.uk).

(IS)

12 THE LUTON BAND

The Luton Band well merits a complete book on its own, but in this history, covering Dunstable & District – a brief but essential reference is more appropriate. It is not to be inferred that Luton is a 'District of Dunstable' of course, but, as a neighbour and having produced one of the top Brass Bands in the country, the Luton Band certainly deserves to be covered. It began as 'The Luton Red Cross Silver Prize Band'. The 'Review' booklet, published in 1907, contains a detailed history of the Band and several others in Luton. An edited extract is detailed in the following pages.

This advertisement appears in the 1907 Review booklet – describing the Band as 'Champions of the South', and 'any number of performers from 12 to 28'!

The inclusion of the words 'Red Cross' in their title was to last until on one particular occasion the members were asked to make use of their (assumed) red cross first aid capabilities, only to find that no-one was able to help. The 'Red Cross' part of their title was accordingly dropped! It may be assumed that this also applied to the Junior Band as well. The Senior Band had been founded in August 1890. The Junior Band is advertised as being established in 1904.

The Luton Red Cross Silver Prize Band c.1906
The picture opposite of the Luton Band appears in the Review Booklet of 1907, referred to in the chapters on the Dunstable Excelsior Silver Prize Band, and the Dunstable Borough Band. The booklet reviewed Bands in Luton & district, of which no less than eight were in Luton. The others included bands in Barton, Hitchin, Stotfold and Stevenage. The author commented that 'Brass Band music

THE LUTON RED CROSS SILVER PRIZE BAND c.1906

The picture above shows a complement of some 28 persons in total, including the Conductor, Mr. T. Cannon, fronted by a display of some of their trophies.

is taking such a prominent place in Luton and surrounding areas . . . it is only of late years that brass band music has assumed such a prominent position in our midst . . . '

The Band, later known simply as 'The Luton Band' was to become one of the leading Brass Bands in the country, a status much due to the Mortimer family (from the Black Dyke Mills Band) – leading musicians of the day who came South to join the Band, with Harry Mortimer becoming a household name, conducting the Band on BBC broadcasts amongst other things. He was much in demand in the Luton–Dunstable area, as well as nationally and internationally.

The Luton Band after 1907

An article in the local Press in the mid 1980s celebrated the Band's 100th anniversary, and traced the origins of the Band to the Luton Ashton Street Mission Band which was formed in 1883. This Band was not referred to in the 1907 booklet where the origins of the Luton Band were solely attributed to the Red Cross Band. However, a section in the booklet on the then Luton Wesleyan Central Mission Band, formed c1882, does clarify things, whereby most of the Ashton St. Mission Band members left in the 1880s to become the nucleus of the Red Cross Band, as the Mission Band 'was not allowed to take part in competitions'.

The Ashton St. members remaining then became the Wesleyan Band. The later history of that band is not, so far, to hand. There has always been a flow of musicians between bands, and whole families were often involved. An early bandmaster of the Wesleyan Band was a Mr. H Cannon; that surname reappears later under Mr. T. Cannon, conductor of the Luton Band, as per the advert shown earlier.

It would seem therefore that 1983 may be taken as the 100th anniversary of the Luton Band. The article refers to the occasion when they won the National Band Competition in 1923 at the Crystal Palace (pictured below outside Luton Museum).

WINNERS OF THE NATIONAL BAND COMPETITION 1923

(M

This was received with great acclaim in the town, with crowds waiting to greet the band at the railway station around midnight on the triumphal day. The article mentions a book about the Band by Mr. Fred Baker, (75 years old at the date of the item), who was present at the contest; he later became a horn player in the Band. The Band here included Harry Mortimer, bandmaster and cornet, Mr. C. Sharp! Albert Coupe, Ted Carter, Percy Osbourne, Fred Green and P. Wildman.

Two Vintage Photos from The Band's 2002 Web Site

Opposite above is the original Ashton Street Luton Mission Band. It was from this band that a breakaway section became the Luton Red Cross Band, later still to become simply the Luton Band. The date is recorded as 1898. Twenty-two members are pictured here, 21 men and one lady. There appears to be a large lantern on a pole on each side of the group, an interesting feature!

Opposite below, the Band in the 1920s with thirty members in full uniform and a selection of trophies centre front, pictured at Stockwood House, Luton.

THE ASHTON STREET LUTON MISSION BAND 1898

(JC)

THE BAND IN THE 1920s

(JC)

THE BAND AT AN OUTDOOR REHEARSAL IN JUNE 1947

The photo was taken by the well known Luton News photographer for many years, the late George Gurney, and was reproduced as a tribute, in the News / Gazette of 18th June 1987.

This scene shows twenty or so members of the Luton Band rehearsing in the yard of the 'Crown & Anchor' in Bridge Street. It was a June day in the long hot summer of 1947, and the thought of playing in their usual room over the stables was a little too much – some refreshing pints can just be seen on the table at bottom left – but only for the customers watching and listening to this first class band.

The band of course was not known as a temperance band, and all bandsmen need a supply of liquid refreshment of some kind, but they were all too busy concentrating on the music when the photo was taken. Their conductor at this time was Mr. Albert Coupe, as seen in the picture. The buildings have long since been demolished.

The Band issued an advertising leaflet in the mid 1970s when the Musical Director was Mr. Lyn Morgan, a distinguished musician and conductor. The leaflet also refers to their professional, Prof. Hargreaves, 'internationally recognised as one of the foremost teachers in the brass band world'. The 1923 event is also described as the 'World and National' Championship – and achieved this status under Mr. William Halliwell.

In 1972, under the directorship of Mr. Albert Coupe M.B.E., the Band won first prize in the W.D. & H.O. Wills British Championships at the Royal Albert Hall. The Secretary during this period was Mr. D.A. Stillwell of Caddington. The leaflet draws attention to the self-supporting nature of the Band, with its members being drawn from a wide cross-section of the community. The Band often included players from Dunstable (and elsewhere). Amongst these players

AC-DELCO 1973

(JC)

This is another photo from the web site, showing The Luton Band at an AC-Delco concert in Dunstable in November 1973. The members present are as listed below:

Top Row: L–R: A. Ritchie, E. Capron, R. Tapsell, T. Wiles, K. Brightman, W. Hill, K. Boyes, D. Taylor.
Middle Row: L–R: D. Baron*, R. Pierce, R. Garrett, D. Henderson, B. Lewis, D. Stillwell, D. Lake, R. Huxtable, P. Cooper, N. Jones.
Bottom Row: L–R: M. Stacey, R. Burnham, K. Bootland, M. Gaddesden, Albert Coupe MBE, D. Morriss, R. Borrie, E. White, T. Papps.

*Mr. David Baron later became conductor in the nineteen-eighties.

THE LUTON BAND IN THEIR ANNIVERSARY YEAR 1983

This photograph of the 1983 Band appeared with the Centenary Article, although no names were provided.

were Messrs. Jim Bull and Bert Poulton of the Dunstable Excelsior Band, who appeared on many occasions both generally and in contests. The Band has always been known for their many broadcasts on the BBC, and have made several recordings over the years. It has been featured on many occasions in concerts in halls and parks locally, including the Sunday afternoon Band Concerts in Dunstable.

THE BAND PICTURED IN 1996

(JC)

The photograph above, taken in 1996, portrays twenty eight players. In the following years the numbers were to diminish, with a low point in the year 2000 of 8 regular players – however things have improved since then with thirteen in 2001. It is hoped that this will herald a greater revival as the new millennium progresses.

The picture is another from the web site, which is mainly in colour. The Site is well worth a visit, containing a wealth of information about the Band's many recordings, personalities, activities and the various combinations in which the Band may be booked and so on.

13 DUNSTABLE SCHOOL ARMY CADET CORPS BAND

The School Cadet Corps began in 1903, with the Drum & Bugle Band being introduced in 1919, and continued until after the Second World War. From 1931 to 1939, an Old Boys section was added to their ranks and the band was in wide demand in the 1930s. The brothers Frank and John Dandy at one time produced a booklet on the band's history. Their names and that of B. W. Squires are always mentioned by Old Boys as leading figures in the life of the Corps and the Band.

A comprehensive collection of photos and documents to the year 1937, collected by Mr. John Dandy, is held by the County Council Archivist. A brief history of the Corps and the Band is also to be found in a history of Dunstable (Grammar) School by Mr. F. M. Bancroft, recently updated, expanded and re-published by The Book Castle.

THE DUNSTABLE SCHOOL ARMY CADET CORPS BAND c.1930

(S& MB)

This picture above is thought to have been taken in 1930 or 1931, and shows the Band as 25 strong. Douglas Darby recognises it to have been taken at the rear of Ashton Lodge in the school grounds.

DUNSTABLE SCHOOL ARMY CADET CORPS & BAND – 10TH MAY 1938

(DC

The Corps and Band pause on their way to the Priory Church for a special Service on the 10th May 1938. The Corps and Band were particularly active between the two world wars.

The old buildings in High Street North can be seen in the background near the junction with Church Street. Nowadays the Nat West Bank would form the immediate backdrop for the picture.

The Dunstable School Army Cadet Corps was headed for many years by A.C. Wadsworth, who was a senior (history) master at the school and in his role as Colonel was in charge of the Corps in both pre-war and post-war periods.

At one time it looked as if the Band would graduate to a full Brass Band when a set of brass instruments was acquired in 1944 and training was introduced. However, when the school was transferred to the Local Education Authority after the war, the school was unable to retain the services of their musical director (Sgt-Major Murphy) and the band reverted to its original drum and bugle format.

DUNSTABLE SCHOOL ARMY CADET CORPS & BAND NOVEMBER 1938

(DG)
(DD)

The Corps can again be seen above marching to the Priory Church in November 1938 to celebrate Remembrance Day, led by the Drum and Bugle band. The photograph from the 'Gazette' shows the Band & Corps proceeding down Church Street, approaching the turning to the Church.

This scene would virtually be unchanged until the late 1960s when the road was widened and all these buildings demolished, to be replaced by the NatWest Bank, the Quadrant, the 'Winston Churchill' and so on. The picture was featured in the 15th September 1988 issue as one of the 'George Gurney Photo File' series. It was loaned to the paper by Mr. John Dandy from his extensive collection.

The Band is led above by Drum Major Ben Squires. He became a fighter pilot in the Second World War, (only a year away), and was tragically killed when he was shot down over the Dutch coast. The shop in the mid-centre of the picture (with the white bay window above), was Stubbs fish and chip shop, the 'modern' frontage six doors up being that of Bakers' furniture shop.

DUNSTABLE SCHOOL ARMY CADETS OUTING, LATE 1930s

This photograph comes from the Dunstable School archive held by its
successor, Manshead School, and is included by courtesy of the headmaster
Mr. Ian Greenley. It has no information on the reverse, but would appear to be
taken in the late nineteen thirties. The background other than the 'bus
provides few clues as to its location, and as the picture is taken against the
vehicle it could have been at the outing's destination, again not known.

There are 47 members in the frame, with 19 drums and 2 cymbals placed at
the front. There are 16 buglers with instruments in the front row, and the
diagonal belts worn by 9 members in the second row indicates they play the
heavier drums including the bass drum, centre. The notice in the 'bus
windows proclaim the Cadet Corps Band, but probably most of the other
cadets in the photo are not bandsmen, but form the rest of the Corps.

THE DUNSTABLE SCHOOL ARMY CADETS IN 1948 AND 1949

This photograph shows the Dunstable School Army Cadet Corps Drum and Bugle Band, taking part in a marching display before the start of a Schoolboys' International football match held in 1948 at Luton Town F.C.'s football ground in Kenilworth Road. This photo, and the one below, were supplied by Mr. Alan Higgs who as a schoolboy was a drummer in the Band. He can be seen centre left (as one of the youngest members, being somewhat less tall than those around him).

Left, the Band leading the Carnival Procession for the Old People's Fete in 1949. They can be seen here in Great Northern Road. Proceeds in those days were usually for 'Cordova' in West Street. Many of the same members can be seen in both pictures, but there appear to be a few changes.

THE DUNSTABLE ARMY CADET CORPS BAND IN 1955

(DG

Another well-established town corps, the Dunstable Army Cadet Corps (as distinct from the Grammar School Corps) in Church Street, in May 1955 on the way to the Priory Church for the Mayor's Sunday parade. This rare picture was printed in the Gazette of 27 Aug 1997, another in the series entitled 'Memories Are Made Of This'. A copy is also in the 'Photo 2000' collection. It featured Mr. Reg. Fowler of Aldbanks and Gerald Nash. Also mentioned were: Stephen Fowler, now in Australia, & Kenneth Fowler (Reg's brothers), Johnny Jones, leading the Band, and David Cropper, with Inspector John leading the procession. The background to the scene is little changed from the earlier photo from 1938.

The picture had been published in the Gazette's 'Yesteryear' series and led Reg Fowler, with Johnny Jones pictured on the left, to contact the paper and supply the details above, and more besides.

ORCHESTRAS

DANCE BANDS

AND

THE JAZZ SCENE

14 ORCHESTRAS

Dunstable's first local newspaper, 'The Dunstable Chronicle', founded in 1855 carried many reports of events which incorporated brass and military bands. There were also often references to other musical activities and 'acts', but rarely anything that would merit the term 'orchestra', although the term 'band' may often have referred to a group other than a brass or military band. The advent of the railways in the earlier to mid part of the century of course meant that various groups of musicians and entertainers travelled into and out of the area regularly.

Tommy Dea's Orchestra

However, prior to the founding of the Wesleyan Men's Bible Class Orchestra, (the BCO) in 1898, there probably had been only one, smaller orchestral ensemble as such in Dunstable (excluding brass and military bands), that of *Mr. Tommy Dea*, who was later to found the BCO. The author had an uncle Mr. Percy Trory who was a pupil of Mr. Dea in the 1910s. (A picture of him with his violin is included later, in the Bible Class Orchestra chapter.)

Mr. Trory often used to speak of *Tommy Dea's Orchestra* in which he played for a while as a student. They used to rehearse and play occasional concerts during this period (the students, Mr. Dea, and other players). It is clear that Tommy Dea must have organised various ensembles or orchestras for some time prior to 1898 although it is not known for how long. It is fairly certain that the musicians from which he started the BCO must have been recruited from his orchestral associates and pupils.

For several decades prior to this time, however, there would have often been small ensembles of musicians assembled together for special occasions and in local churches to play for services where no organ was available, or to support a special event in the church.

(Tommy Dea's contribution to the founding of the Bible Class Orchestra, (see that chapter), and its continued success was later to be warmly acknowledged on the occasion of the Bible Class's Jubilee publication in 1936, the 38th anniversary of the Orchestra, in which he is described as still playing).

Waterlow & Sons Orchestra – 'WASO'

Another orchestra was to be founded in the early years of the 20th century, that of the firm of Waterlow and Sons the printers. Waterlows had come to Dunstable from London in 1891, bringing much needed employment to the town, and also bringing employees from its London base. The orchestra however was not formed until some time after the end of the first world war, the actual date still to be confirmed.

'WASO' – (The Waterlow & Sons Orchestra) – became well established and not surprisingly included in its ranks players from other groups including the BCO! It was conducted for many years by Mr. Cyril Carter, violin, also a prominent member of the BCO. Other players included Eddie Hansen, percussion (also clarinet), Fred Janes, brass, who was later to lead his own dance band, Charlie Young, percussion, Percy Trory, violin, and also on violin –

unsurprisingly, Tommy Dea. It is worth mentioning here that Mr. Dea and his daughter Florrie often used to take part in local concerts at the town hall and elsewhere, as a duo and with other musicians. Florrie Dea has been described by Douglas Darby as a first class cellist of outstanding ability.

Although WASO performed at several venues, Waterlows had its own canteen on the premises, with a stage, dance floor, and of course catering facilities, in which the orchestra – or its smaller dance band version (WASSA – the Waterlows Athletic, Sports & Social Association band) performed. Outside organisations could also hire the canteen. The Firm also had its own 11-acre sports ground, between AC-Delco and French's Avenue, which contained a fair-sized pavilion for use in various sports activities, but was itself capable of holding dances and other functions. Unfortunately, the sports ground site has now been disposed of for redevelopment, and the pavilion demolished.

The Waterlows Printing Works itself was closed in 1991, apart from a small residual business in the Woodside estate, when Robert Maxwell's B.P.C., of which Waterlows became a part, was restructured some years ago. The old works site now boasts an attractive housing estate. The Orchestra however had closed down many years before this, the precise date to be determined, but it was probably in the late thirties.

It was from the ranks of 'WASO' that the 'Fred Janes Dance Band' and, the 'Embassy Dance Band' were later formed, adding musicians such as Bill Harris, a gifted local pianist, and others. Dance bands have a separate chapter later on.

The Congregational Church Orchestra

The Congregational Orchestra was formed in Edward Street, in the inter-war years and we are fortunate to have this picture (opposite above) of the orchestra taken around 1930.

The actual date of the photo is not known, but it must have been in the summertime in the early thirties and taken out of doors. The piano must have taken some man-handling and might well have been knocked out of tune! The premises in Edward Street have since been modernised while keeping the original architecture of the building intact (the original Church had to be demolished). The current building was in fact the old school house. The description has also been changed to the United Reformed Church, but many older Dunstablians still remember it as 'The Congry'.

The Dunstable Amateur Operatic & Dramatic Society

The 'Twenties' also saw the founding of the *Dunstable Amateur Operatic and Dramatic Society*, and an Orchestra was put together to play for their various performances in the town. Douglas Darby recalls the Musical Director and Producer for many years being Mr. Arthur Childs (no relation to Mr. John Childs who conducted the Bible Class Orchestra in later years). Other members included George Parsons violin, Eddie Hanson, drums etc. and Kit Darby.

Douglas Darby recalls that this first Operatic (and Dramatic) Society and its Orchestra, with varying line-ups, lasted from the twenties to the late fifties, when it appears to have been wound up in its then form. However it was later to be succeeded by a newly instituted organisation. The re-instituted (& current) *Dunstable Amateur Operatic & Dramatic Society* was started after the *1963 Pageant of Dunstable* by the Rev. Rupert Child, of the Priory Church, (who had

THE CONGREGATIONAL CHURCH ORCHESTRA c.1930

The full line-up is identified. The group comprises six strings, piano and clarinet; the gentleman with the clarinet at bottom left actually playing the concertina when this picture was taken. (PB. DD)
The musicians are: Top row L–R: Mrs. Draper (piano), Lawrence Procter, Aubrey Stanbridge, and Alec Goodwin (violins). Bottom row L–R: Mr. Barber, (clarinet and concertina), Mary Sharratt, Doris Bye and Mrs. Allen (violins).

THE DUNSTABLE AMATEUR OPERATIC & DRAMATIC SOCIETY 1927

A Scene From the Society's production of 'Tom Jones' in 1927.

played the continuity role of the Ballad Singer in the Pageant), together with Mr. Haydn Parrott. It was about this time that the new Civic Hall was built to provide new facilities for a range of activities, opening in 1964 to begin its 37 years of existence, and the Society saw opportunities for success in this futuristic new hall.

Douglas also recalls their first production, 'Trial By Jury', actually being presented in the Speech Hall of Dunstable Grammar School in 1963, before moving to the new Civic Hall in the following year. He remembers the orchestras being ad hoc line-ups for each production but mentioned Kenny Boyes (trumpet), John Tournay (percussion), Chris Horrell (bass) & Kitty Darby. Douglas recalled that his mother & father had also sung in the original society. Of course many others also took part in both societies. This second body has produced many performances in the period up to the present day, including Musicals, Concerts, & Shows, in addition to the more traditional Operatic material.

THE DUNSTABLE AMATEUR OPERATIC & DRAMATIC SOCIETY 1998

The DAODS production of 'Crazy for You' in November 1998.

The Gazette, dated 11th November 1998 published this energetic picture of the DAODS production of 'Crazy for You'. The whole performance was warmly received, although the venue, did not appear to be mentioned on this occasion, as neither was the musical accompaniment, although we can see a clarinettist bottom left, and a conductor's baton, right, raised above the brass player. It is clear that a great deal of preparation and effort went into the production.

The DAODS was for many years led by Miss Grace Mackintosh as Musical Director. Miss Mackintosh was Head of Music at Queen Eleanor's School at the time (later to merge with Kingsbury School to form Queensbury School). Other Musical Directors who followed, were Mrs. Phillida Driver, Mr. Terry Driver, Mr. John Fryer, Ms. Jane Hills and presently Miss Joe Burton.

Many excellent shows have been presented to local audiences over the years, including 'Crazy for You' (overleaf), 'Pirates of Penzance', 'Carmen', 'My Fair Lady', 'Guys & Dolls', and 'Fiddler on the Roof'. These and other productions were staged initially at the Queensway Hall, then Manshead School, with more recently Queensbury School becoming a regular venue. The last production at the Queensway Hall was 'Me & My Gal'.

The Orchestra has always been of the best quality, although still basically 'ad hoc' for each occasion, but containing regular stalwarts over the years. These include Terry Driver (violin), John Tournay (percussion), Andy Stewart (clarinet & saxophone), Anne Parrott (violin), Julie Jay (cello), Chris Pettit (reeds), Ken Boyes (trumpet) and Ian Grant (trumpet).

The Society, presented a production of 'Hello Dolly' in December 2002, and had started rehearsals for 'Half a Sixpence', due in the spring of 2003, with future plans for 'Kiss Me Kate' and 'South Pacific'. In the meantime, their Christmas concert for 2002 took place at the 'Little Theatre'. So the Society continues to flourish in the new millennium, with secretary Mr. Stan Woodhouse the person to contact.

The Dunstable Three Arts Society

This Society began life in the early inter war years, the early nineteen-twenties in fact. The Town Guide for 1933 records the latest musical " The Belle Of New York" (1932) as the tenth production, staged as usual at the Palace Theatre, Dunstable. The musical director was Mr. Percy Bass, headmaster at the Ashton School; the president, Dr. A. Mcleod; treasurer Mr. A. Scott; and the secretary, Mr. G. Tomlin.

This being the tenth in the series should indicate that the society must have started at least in 1922. Drama, together with musical productions represented only one (or two) of the Arts, however. The third has so far not been defined!

The Town Guide for 1937 informs us that the thirteenth production in the series, that of the 'Student Prince', was

THE PALACE THEATRE, DUNSTABLE

The 'Palace' theatre, left, was a stylish building next to the Union Cinema in High Street North. After the war, however, it became disused and was demolished.

produced (in 1936) by Mr. A. Wallis, with an orchestra conducted by Mr. H. Field, again at the Palace Theatre. Mr. Wallis was widely acknowledged as the main impetus behind the Society.

The Town Guides for 1939 and after no longer mention the Society. The onset of World War II may well have rendered its continuation impossible.

The Adult School

This was another well established organisation that flourished during the inter-war years. As its name implies it provided educational opportunities to adults in the town and also included a drama group called the 'Adult School Players'. Its repertoire however included comic opera, and the Gazette of the 20th February 1935 featured a report and pictures of the Adult School Operatic Society's production of 'San Marino'.

There is no mention of its musical backing, though (not an uncommon occurrence!). It is possible that Cyril Carter's own orchestra might have played for the production as his orchestra was formed to play for a range of organisations in Dunstable. Each occasion would find many familiar faces in the line-up. The Adult School however was founded for a range of subjects and it would seem that music and drama may have only been an occasional activity.

The Inter-War Years 1919–1939

The years between the wars was a period when the 'wireless' or radio was to become a common feature in the average household. Television, first introduced in 1936 to a very restricted area in and around the London area, was unable to spread more widely until after the second world war, and was not yet a part of everyday life. It was a period in which several new organisations flourished in Dunstable. In addition to the musical bodies in this review, Dunstable had a Literary and Scientific Society. The WEA was active in the town and had a drama group, but no music classes were advertised.

Of course the cinema was becoming more and more popular as technology progressed and the silent film with its local piano-accompanist was becoming replaced by the 'Talkies', which featured recorded music, played by large orchestras to a high professional standard. Recorded music became more and more available in the form of the 78 rpm shellac disc, but which however only allowed a three minute version of music (and comedy dissertations) to be recorded in its common ten inch format. This increase in available music of all kinds was to provide bands and orchestras with a wider variety of material to perform. Local music shops were keen to supply copies of the latest popular records as broadcast on the radio, and more besides. Many shops also supplied pianos and other instruments to an increasingly aware and enthusiastic public. Older Dunstablians will remember Messrs. Farmers of Church Street, who were advertising 'radios & pianos' in the 1933 Dunstable Town Guide. They also supplied records, sheet music, and other products, enabling the local populace to play the latest 'hits', and the classics, on their pianos. Almost everyone possessed a piano in those days.

15 THE BIBLE CLASS ORCHESTRA

The Wesleyan Bible Class, The Square

The Wesleyan Bible Class started as a link between senior Sunday School and the senior church. The first steps to its formation were in 1884, when the Young Men's Bible Class was formed for boys around 14 years of age. An organisation for older boys was then formed in March 1886 by the late Mr. T. Weatherill. It was immediately expanded to include men of all ages and re-named the 'Men's Bible Class'. Mr. Weatherill led it for 38 years and it became an enduring success. The Class actually met at the Methodist Institute in Chapel Walk roughly where Wilkinson's store now stands, opposite the side entrance to the church.

The Orchestra was introduced in 1898 primarily to provide music for the activities of the Bible Class, to play for hymns, anthems and solo accompaniments. However its repertoire has never been confined to that role alone. From the early times it has played a wide range of orchestral music, albeit compatible with its roots in the Bible Class.

The regular weekly meetings were supported by the orchestra and pianists in the religious music scheduled for the particular day. The expansion of its repertoire was largely given scope in the monthly Band Sundays when the orchestra was at its most numerous and when guest players and singers were added to its ranks. Several ladies also frequently joined with the men's orchestra. A typical programme for the late 'fifties is illustrated on a later page. It was on those Band Sundays that members of the Excelsior Brass Band came along to add to the number and scope of the orchestra including members of the Dolman family, in particular Mr. William Dolman who was to play a leading role as conductor for many years after Tommy Dea.

THE BIBLE CLASS MEMBERS 1892

This photo of the Bible Class members in 1892, (this is not the Orchestra), was included in the 1936 Jubilee Booklet.

THE WESLEYAN BIBLE CLASS ORCHESTRA, THE SQUARE IN 1910

The picture above is taken from the 1936 Jubilee Booklet of the Men's Bible Class. A full-size original has so far not been found, only the small segment described on the next page. The photo was taken in 1910, twelve years after the Orchestra was founded. The segment referred to, with the three persons shown can clearly be seen to have come from the lower middle-right of the group above, including the conductor William Dolman.

The full group above comprises 25 musicians, of whom eight are ladies. The ladies had had their own bible class for some time by then (after the men's class was founded in 1886) but did not form an orchestra of their own; however they joined with the men on frequent occasions, as of course on the occasion of this photograph. Apart from the three musicians in the segment opposite, the full identification of the 1910 group has still to be completed.

The small segment of the original photograph (opposite) has obviously been cut from an original, probably for one or other of the persons depicted. It is likely that other segments may exist.

If a complete copy can be found, it would be a minor treasure as the photo is obviously of a high standard. The segment portrays the Conductor, Mr. William Dolman with his own instrument at his feet, with to his left, the cellist Mrs. Elsie Proverbs, and the viola or violinist, Mrs. Freeman, on her left.

Members in the 1898 & 1936 orchestras are set out opposite – this may help in the naming of the 1910 group.

THE BIBLE CLASS ORCHESTRA IN 1910 (PART)

The 15 Orchestra Members in 1898 (inc 1 lady):	
Conductor	Mr. Tommy Dea
Double Bass	Mr. W. Dolman
Violins	T. Dea
	B. White
	A. Groom
	W. Jones
	W. Humphrey
	J. Barratt
	G. Banwell
	J. Picton
Flute	A. Bunker
Piccolo	F. Dolemore
Clarinet	A. Sinfield
Cornet	F. Summerfield
Cello	W. Goode
Piano or Organ	Miss F. Bull

The 25 Orchestra Members in 1936 (inc 4 ladies):			
Conductor	Mr. W. Dolman	Viola	R. Pearce
Double Basses	A. Groom, V. Field	Cello	S. C. Bell
Violins	T. Dea (leader)	Trumpets	W. Matthews
	Mrs. F. Rogers		J. Bull
	Mrs. S. Freeman		
	Mrs. Watson	Flute	H. Field
	G. Parsons	Percussion	K. Bayliss
	C. Carter	Pianists	Miss A. Pearce
	B. Poulton		W. Tibbett
	N. Bates		
	J. Duncan		
	H. Lansdowne		
	R. Gray		
	S. Freeman		
	A. Goodwin		
	S. West		

PEACE CELEBRATIONS 19TH JULY 1919 – SERVICE AT THE 'SQUARE'

This photograph comes from the Victory Souvenir Booklet issued by a local Committee to mark the Town's Peace Celebrations on 19th July 1919. It depicts a Service on the Square, which took place at 10.00 a.m. outside the Methodist Church, conducted by the Rev. Canon Baker of the Priory Church, with other local clergy leading various sections of the proceedings. Note the old buildings to the right.

The Service was followed by a Choral Concert with a massed choir drawn from the local churches and others. It was 'accompanied by an Orchestra', which would have been made up of members of the Bible Class Orchestra, the Excelsior Brass Band & possibly others including members of the Borough Band. Some of the musical proceedings were arranged by Mr. Arthur Davis later to become well known as the conductor of the world-famous Luton Girls Choir. The Conductor overall was Mr. Harold Deacon, organist & choirmaster at the Priory Church. The Event was organised by a 'Musical Committee', the chairman of which was Mr. A. Boskett, Secretary Mr.H.J. Darby, with the committee including Messrs. A. E. Bunker, W. Small, A. Potton, C. Cook, G. Purcell, H. Sloan and last but not least, Mr. William Dolman, conductor of the BCO and the Excelsior. More details of that day's many events can be found in the chapter on the Excelsior Band.

Percy Trory – Violin

This photograph of Mr. Percy Trory with his violin was taken in the late 1910s in the garden of the family home in Chiltern Road next to the former Chiltern Road School. He was a pupil of Mr. Tommy Dea for many years, often playing with Mr. Dea's Orchestra, which used to meet at the then Congregational Church in Edward Street, now the United Reformed Church. He later played with the Bible Class Orchestra during the period from the late 'forties to the early 'sixties.

The Author, a nephew of Mr. Trory, has vivid memories in his early teens, of attending a concert by the BCO at the Priory Parish Hall, in which his uncle was playing (a near neighbour of Percy's, Mr. Vince Bachini, was also present on violin).

The occasion was probably a Harvest Festival – and their rendition of the tune 'Stanchen' left a particular impression. Douglas Darby recalls this particular tune as a great favourite, especially with the ladies at the Baptist Church, Houghton Regis' Harvest Festival, where they liked to tap their spoons to the music!

Later on Percy suffered a mild stroke, which left him unable to play demanding material, although he was eventually able to play slow ballads at family get-togethers and so on. He died in 1977 aged 71 years. He was married to Winifred Hucklesby from Luton, and had one son, Philip, now living with his family in Canada.

The Choral Union

The Orchestra still continued with its regular Sunday meetings & Band Sundays throughout the twenties and thirties, but combined these with performances on the Methodist Circuit and at other venues, particularly for Harvest festivals. These were a popular feature of its annual 'extra-mural' activities not only at Nonconformist venues, but elsewhere including the Priory Parish Hall. The thirties however was a more expansive period for the orchestra. It was featured prominently in a number of annual performances of the major Oratorios held at the 'Square' in conjunction with the newly-formed *Dunstable Choral Union*.

THE BIBLE CLASS ORCHESTRA AND THE CHORAL UNION AT REHEARSAL

The united choirs and the Square Men's Bible Class Orchestra are pictured at a rehearsal of one of the great Oratorios, 'The Creation' or 'The Messiah', in the early 1930s. (Photo, Luton News)

The Orchestra is deployed at the front of the ensemble on 'stage' at the Methodist Church, the Square, Dunstable. The organist can be seen at the middle-upper part of the photo with an assistant to his right, facing the main section of the choir, with the array of organ pipes at the rear of the Church.

The musicians taking part will be mainly those identified in the 1936 Jubilee Booklet, with the Conductor certain to be Mr. William Dolman.

The Choral Union was formed in 1930 from members of the Nonconformist Church choirs of the town, together with friends and associates. Its sole object was the rendering of Oratorios to the highest standard they could achieve, and to support the introduction of high-class soloists. These included the misses Elsie Suddaby and Flora Woodman, & Messrs. Edward Reach, Horace Stevens, Kenneth Ellis & Robert Easton (all well-known performers, many featured on the BBC).

The Choral Union was run by a committee which comprised Messrs. G.W. Parsons, a member of the Orchestra, F. A. Boskett, H. R. N. Sloan, F. Costin, and R. A. Custance. The Performances started in 1930 with 'The Creation', followed in 1931 by 'Elijah' and in 1932, the 'Messiah'. The whole ensemble was conducted by Mr. Leslie Boskett, organist at the 'Square' (and a senior master at the Grammar School, and who was involved with musical productions at the school).

A prominent soloist at the time was Mr. Harry Mortimer, described as 'Solo trumpeter of the Halle Orchestra'. He became still more well-known later as a major figure in the Brass Band movement, and conducted the famous Luton Band for several years along with other engagements for the BBC.

The *Luton Choral Union*, as opposed to the *Dunstable Choral Union*, is later featured in the Gazette of 1936, and may have superseded the Dunstable organisation by then as the main forum for the performance of Oratorio locally, as no further reference has so far been found to the Dunstable Choral Union after the early nineteen-thirties. (Interestingly, the 1933 Dunstable Town Guide includes a reference to *'The First Dunstable Eistedfodd'*, although little or nothing appears to be known of this, unless it actually refers to the Choral Union events).

Other Musical Developments

Members of the orchestra, together with other local musicians, often formed ad hoc ensembles to support events in the town. Then, as always, musicians tended to band together from various disciplines if needed or requested, a prime example being brass players such as William Dolman who in fact took leading roles in all areas of musical activity in the area, and of course Cyril Carter.

The thirties also saw the formation of several dance bands locally, adding to the variety and number of outlets for musicians to play, including BCO members.

Local Operatic organisations also flourished in this period, although Press reports tended not to highlight the musicians taking part. Douglas Darby tells us that there was a separate Operatic Society Orchestra from the twenties to the late fifties, under the musical direction & production of Mr Arthur Childs for many years. More details of the Operatic Society and the orchestra are included in another part of the chapter.

This brings us to the year 1936, the Jubilee year of the Bible Class, formed in 1886, fifty years before, (the Orchestra was formed in 1898 and was a mere thirty-eight years old in 1936).

The eventual Jubilee year of the Orchestra as a separate entity (1948), appears not to have been celebrated, or even referred to (according to current records). Perhaps the date being so close to the end of World War II had something to do with this.

The Bible Class Jubilee Year 1936

The 50th anniversary of the founding in 1886 of the Wesleyan Men's Bible Class was commemorated by amongst other things, a rather splendid Jubilee Brochure, and there exists a well-preserved copy of which the front cover is illustrated overleaf. As well as much information about the Bible Class itself, it includes many references to the Orchestra, founded in 1898.

The main page relating to the Orchestra, page 7, states:

'A development which has largely contributed to the popularity & influence of the Bible Class was the formation of an Orchestra some thirty-eight years ago.

'It is an unqualified delight to set on record that we rejoice to number three of the original members amongst those who today are to be found week by week in their places.

'The loyalty and devotion of our friends Messrs. T. Dea, W. Dolman and A. Groom demands special recognition and acknowledgement'.

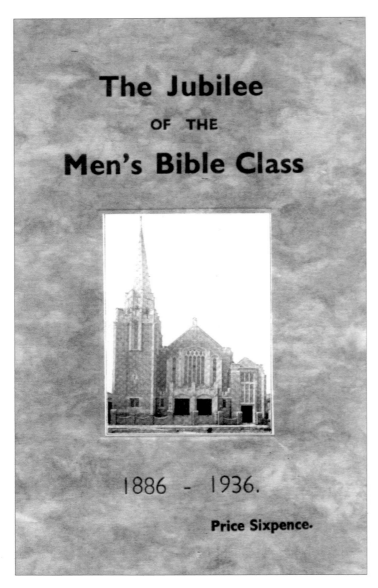

The Jubilee

OF THE

Men's Bible Class

1886 - 1936.

Price Sixpence.

Mr. Dea, who was mainly instrumental in forming an Orchestra so long ago has been good enough to supply a statement which sets out the facts: here it is.

Mr. Dea says; 'The origin of the Wesleyan Bible Class Orchestra was a thought in the mind of Mr. Thomas Weatherill, who first consulted Mr. Arthur Bunker and Mr. Frank Dolemore, both members of the choir. These brethren interviewed me on the project and eventually Mr. Weatherill sent for me and asked me if I would do my best to form such an Orchestra to play in the Bible Class.'

Tommy Dea did just that and the following fifteen are the original players:
Violins: Messrs. B. White,
A. Groom, W. Jones,
W. Humphrey, J. Barret,
T. Dea, G. Banwell, J. Picton.
Flute: W. A. Bunker.
Piccolo: F. Dolemore.
Cornet: F. Summerfield.
Clarinet: A. Sinfield.
Cello: W. Goode.
Double-bass: W. Dolman.
Piano or Organ: Miss F. Bull.

The writer goes on to say: 'Since its formation, the Orchestra has proved an invaluable asset and the quality of the music rendered has made a sustained appeal to all music lovers. In addition, the Orchestral accompaniment of the hymns has resulted in the singing being conspicuously marked by swing, verve, and abandon, and men do love to 'let themselves go' where singing is concerned.

'How largely this has been contributory to the popularity of the actual meetings is impossible to estimate. From time to time competent and accomplished musicians have generously given their help, with the result that the standard of the 'output' has been uniformly high. Under the conductorship of Mr. W. Dolman, the Orchestra is today achieving results which certainly cannot have been surpassed.'

The brochure includes a photo of the Orchestra dated 1910 of which only a small section of the original has been found (as illustrated on an earlier page).

The brochure tells us that Mr. Tommy Dea and Mr. A. Groom were still playing in 1936, and therefore likely to be in the full photo of 1910; that makes five out of twenty-five so far identified. The Orchestra was well represented in these celebrations, but as mentioned earlier does not appear to have had its own Jubilee.

A Portrait of Douglas Darby

Douglas Darby is pictured here with his tenor saxophone in the nineteen thirties. From the 'thirties he had begun a long association with music in Dunstable, interrupted by spells with His Majesty's Forces and career moves away from the town, but always taking the opportunity to play in various groups both in the U.K. and Germany in off duty and leisure hours.

He has particularly been associated with the Wesleyan Men's Bible Class Orchestra where he originally played percussion, switching to his preferred instrument, the saxophone, when he successfully persuaded the conductor at

the time that, as there was a shortage of cellists, he would be able to play the cello role on the tenor sax.

He has played with many other groups including dance bands and orchestras. In recent years he has been associated with the Dunstable Light Concert Orchestra (later the Dunstable Concert Music Society) amongst others.

Today, although retired from active playing, he still owns his soprano saxophone, and is well known as a speaker on musical and local history topics in Dunstable & district and has contributed a great deal to the contents of 'Strike Up The Band.'

The 1930s to the 1950s

Following the Jubilee celebrations in 1936, the Orchestra continued to flourish developing its repertoire and capabilities, and continuing to provide its support for the weekly meetings. The monthly Band Sundays however provided a widening range of music, with many guest musicians joining the Orchestra on a regular basis. This carried on until the early years of the Second World War, 1939,1940,1941.

Inevitably, the demands and circumstances of the war progressively affected the number and ages of the musicians taking part. Tributes had already been paid to the members who had given their lives in the first war – and to that list, further names might be added as the 1939–45 war took its toll. The Orchestra nevertheless was able to continue with a viable line up of instruments during the war years.

At the end of the war, the returning servicemen included members of the Orchestra, and many continued to play throughout the post war years – 1945, '46, '47,and 1948, (its own Jubilee year), although the average age tended to rise as fewer younger people joined its ranks. The immediate post war years carried on the traditions established before the war, with Mr. William Dolman conducting and Mr. Tommy Dea leading as they had done during the war.

Douglas Darby recalls that the Orchestra was kept in shape by regular rehearsals. These had always taken place on Tuesday evenings throughout its long history, both to maintain standards, to prepare for the forthcoming Sundays and also of course for other engagements.

As the 'fifties arrived, the indisposition of William Dolman (and his death in c1951 at the age of 79), the effects of the newly developing television services, and other factors began to make their influences felt.

For the time being however, the Orchestra managed to carry on its traditions with others taking up the leadership roles. (A tribute to Wm. Dolman is included in the chapter on the Excelsior Band). The Orchestra in the 'fifties could be as many as 35 players or as low as 10 or 12 in number. Other names recalled by Doug Darby & Jim Bull are Norman Bates, 2nd violin, Alan Goodwin, who had to give up due to injury, Bill Lee, trumpet, Jim Bull of course on trumpet, and Bill Matthews.

THE ORCHESTRA AT MIDLAND ROAD LUTON

(DD)

This photo was taken in the nineteen-fifties at Midland Road Methodist Church in Luton, and shows members of the Orchestra with its conductor, Mr. John Childs.

The players are as shown below:

Conductor – John Childs

1st. Violins	Cyril Carter (leader)	Clarinet	Arthur Childs
	Cyril Nind	Saxophone	Douglas Darby
	Mr. Freeman	Trumpet	Bill Matthews
	Mrs. Freeman	Trombone	Cyril Watts
2nd Violin	Arthur Thomas	Percussion	Ken Bayliss
Viola	Ron Pearce	Piano	Thelma Fountain
Cellos	Arthur Lewis	Soloist	Brian Matthews
	Chris Horrell	Bass	Arthur Groom

There are actually nineteen persons in the picture, seventeen of whom are identified above as members of the Orchestra.

The 1950s to the 1980s

A typical Sunday afternoon programme of music & other items from a Sunday meeting in the nineteen-fifties is shown here.

SUNDAY   23rd   JULY.

HYMN 634.   Pianist   Mr Shepherd.

Prayer.

Hymn 832.   Pianist.   P.Tillbrook.   (Collection)

Collection Prayer.

Bible Reading.   Psalm 19.

Orchestra. March ON THE QUARTER DECK. Pianist Mr Shepherd.

Vocal Solo   Mrs Clemmitt.   Pianist. Mrs Lakin.

Vocal Solo. Brian Matthews.   Own pianist.

Orchestra.   The Nun's Chorus.   Pianist. Mr Shepherd.

Piano solo.   P.Tillbrook.

Readings ....short stories requested.

Hymn 431   Pianist   Mrs Lakin.

Vocal Solo.   Mrs Clemmitt. Pianist. Mrs Lakin.

Vocal Solo.   Brian Matthews. Own Pianist.

Orchestra.   Selection of Melodies from
             PERCHANCE TO DREAM.   Pianist Mrs Lakin.

Hymn. 108.   Pianist. Mrs Lakin.

Prayer and Vesper 688.

After the war, numbers eventually declined after an initial spurt.

Another BCO musician, Dave Bradley, violin and sax, left for a while and joined the 'Davalan Trio' dance band with Alan Higgs, drums, and Alan Riding, piano. The trio was sometimes augmented with a trumpet, with Douglas Darby on tenor sax, and on occasion appeared with the BCO for a joint concert.

BCO Concerts were often played in the 'fifties & 'sixties on the (second) bandstand at the rear of Grove House Gardens, often using arrangements by Mr. John Childs. The author remembers as a lad waiting for a haircut in Ellis's in West Street, and seeing John Childs writing arrangements for the Orchestra while he waited. (Ellis's old premises were later dismantled and taken to the Chiltern Outdoor Museum where they can be seen today).

Douglas was with the Orchestra when they finally left the Wesleyan premises, transferring to the Waterlow Road Chapel where they played for several years, later calling themselves the 'Dunstable Light Orchestra'. The organist and pianist there was Mr. Derek Bird, also well known for his own contribution to the local music scene over many years.

Cyril Carter – Obituary, and a change for the BCO

This obituary was penned by Mr. Douglas Darby for the local Press and Church magazine. The year and date is not stated in the narrative but is thought to be c.1970. Cyril Carter was also remembered for forming his own orchestra, and for his participation in other ensembles in the town over a great many years.

Cyril Carter who died just before Christmas, will be remembered for his long association with the Orchestra of the former Men's Bible Class. As a regular player for many years, he took over as violin leader just after the war and later became solely responsible for it's musical direction. Under his guidance the Orchestra played regularly every Sunday afternoon and for Services and concerts at many churches in the circuit and charity events in the neighbouring districts.

When the Bible Classes were discontinued at The Square arrangements were made for a move to Waterlow Road and Cyril continued to lead and direct the re-named Dunstable Light Concert Orchestra. His solo items were a popular feature and he also made many personal appearances with other local musicians.

His working life was with Waterlow's and he was responsible for preparation and control of their printing inks. Our sympathy is extended to his widow, Dorothy.

His passing rather symbolised the demise of the Bible Class Orchestra as such, although the orchestra in effect continued in a new format as the Dunstable Light Orchestra after the move initially to The Waterlow Road Methodist Church, then to a new base at Dunstable College as the Dunstable College Music Society Orchestra, later relocating at St. George's School as the Dunstable Concert Music Society Orchestra, led by Mr. Phil Thomas, where they continue to play today.

DUNSTABLE COLLEGE MUSIC SOCIETY ORCHESTRA

(W

1989. The BCO had moved to Dunstable College becoming a combined mixed choir & orchestra as Dunstable College Music Society, later re-formed as below.

DUNSTABLE CONCERT MUSIC SOCIETY ORCHESTRA

(A

Phil Thomas leads the Dunstable Concert Music Society Orchestra at the Old Palace Lodge, at one of the recent annual Tudor Days.

16 DANCE BANDS AND THE JAZZ SCENE

The 'Jazz Age' came to this country from America after the end of the First World War, strongly influenced by a tour of Britain in 1919 by 'The Original Dixieland Jazz Band' from the USA. Local dances up to this time were catered for by either a soloist, probably a pianist, a brass band, or a small orchestra. The type of dances performed up to this time had mainly been the traditional minuets, quadrilles, reels, Viennese waltzes, etc. (The waltz had earlier been blamed for a decline in the minuet and other traditional dances around the end of the 19th century).

The advent of jazz and the robust dance forms it brought with it ('jiving', 'jitterbugging', etc) gave rise to a lot of concern at the time, but although a wide range of other dances managed to survive, things would never be the same again. From the jazz influences came the more 'arranged' swing music, and the advent of *Dance Bands*, still strongly influenced by the U.S.A. Local bands sought to emulate both the American and British dance bands. The ease of travel to London, the development of the 'wireless', the increasing availability of recorded music, and the development of talking pictures bringing the latest in popular music to a wider range of the population.

It may be worth mentioning here that the teaching of the 'tonic sol-fa' method of writing down music ('doh-re-me'), as an aid to notation etc. had been introduced locally by various teachers in Dunstable in lectures from the late 19th cent. The author's father in fact was able to take down the 'latest' tunes in tonic-sol-fa from visits to London shows in the 'twenties & 'thirties and play them with friends in a small local group they had for a while called 'The Bon Five'!

The inter-war years 1919 to 1939 saw a number of dance bands in the Dunstable area. The predominant influences were still from American bands and this would continue throughout the 2nd World War with the arrival in the U.K. of *Glenn Miller and his Orchestra* in army uniform. The Miller Band made many broadcasts on the BBC, often from studios in Bedford.

The war was to remove many younger men from the national and local scene as they were called up for active service. However, some of the older musicians remained and local dances with local bands thrived during wartime, and just as local brass players played in various local orchestras, so many also could be seen in dance and jazz bands, together with up and coming younger players. Servicemen also managed to continue their musical activities in both military bands and service dance bands. The post-war period, with the return of servicemen to civilian life, and the rising generation, led to a period of great activity in the dance band and jazz fields in the country, until the mid 1960s, when Rock & Roll, the Beatles and the advent of the 'Disco' etc. were to have a far reaching effect on the jazz and local dance scene.

The Geoff Stokes Orchestra
Geoff Stokes was a well known Bandleader in the Dunstable–Luton area from the early nineteen-thirties to the nineteen-fifties. He formed his first band in the heyday of the dance craze that swept the country.

THE GEOFF STOKES ORCHESTRA OF 1933

(MD
JB)

Left to Right – Geoff Stokes, Clarinet, Tenor, Alto & Soprano Saxophones; Bill Dolman, Violin; Ken Bayliss, Drums; Bert Poulton, Trumpet.

The band included two players from The Excelsior Band, but was not always limited to four musicians. The above group represented a viable and versatile line-up for dances in the early thirties. The drum kit was typical of that early period, with the large bass drum, the absence of a 'hi-hat', (the double cymbal operated by a pedal on a telescopic stand), the small single cymbals suspended from a single bar, and the absence of tom-toms. The band typified the wide range of groups that individual musicians played for. Readers will be aware of this from other chapters, as exemplified by the inclusion above of William (Bill) Dolman in particular!

The nineteen-thirties was a period when economic and technological developments were expanding the horizons of almost everyone in the country. More money to spend, the expansion of radio, cinema and the then modern '78' recordings of popular bands, and modern ballroom dancing, brought large crowds to many local venues on a Saturday night to dance the night away, until midnight anyway.

The photograph opposite above is clearly taken from the position of the band on the stage at the Town Hall. We can see music stands at the lower edge of the photo, and the circular object, lower mid-left, is a microphone of that era, probably the only one in use on the stage. In those days, microphones were basically for public announcements and to slightly amplify the sound of the music. The modern use of several 'mikes' to amplify individuals, (mixed and processed), was not yet an available option.

N.B. Intriguingly, the 1940–41 Town Guide mentions an otherwise little-known group, Wesley Lee and his New St Louis Players Dance Orchestra.

A DANCE AT THE OLD DUNSTABLE TOWN HALL IN HIGH STREET NORTH IN 1935

(DG)

The picture was provided for the 'Gazette' by Mr. Ledger of Drovers Way who informed the paper that his sister was in the photo, and that many shops in the town were open until 10.00 p.m. on a Saturday evening!

THE DAVALAN DANCE BAND IN THE FIFTIES

(DD)

The picture was taken during a dinner-dance engagement in the mid nineteen fifties. The venue is believed to be in the function room at the 'Warden Tavern' in Luton.

The Davalan Dance Band in the Fifties

The Davalan Trio was a well known dance band in Dunstable and Luton in the nineteen-fifties -sixties period. The Trio consisted of David Bradley (of the BCO) on tenor saxophone, Alan Riding on piano, and Alan Higgs on drums. (The one Dave & two Alans giving the Trio its name). The photograph shows the Trio augmented to a Quintet – The Davalan Quintet. On this occasion the Trio was joined by Douglas Darby (2nd right), also on tenor saxophone, and a trumpet player still to be identified.

The period was prolific for live musicians everywhere, and the local Dunstable–Luton scene was no exception. In those days many personal or family celebrations would take place at local venues and local musicians would be engaged. Local businesses would have an annual Christmas 'do' for their employees often in the form of a dinner-dance. Bands would play a wide range of material to suit all ages and this became an accepted routine, with each age group catered for. Games would also be played! often compered by the bandleader, as would be the whole evening. Larger functions of course would take place in bigger venues which were more often compered by a Toastmaster or 'Redcoat'.

Kenny Ball and his Jazz Band visit Dunstable

The author remembers being able to persuade the organisers of the Priory Church Fete to book the Kenny Ball Band as an attraction for jazz fans generally, the younger generation in particular, and the author! 1962 was still part of the post war jazz revival including British 'Trad', and this was probably the leading band of its style in the country. The band was a great success and was well received. 'Rock & Roll', the 'Beatles', etc would soon have what was to be a subduing effect on jazz and other popular music, although jazz fans managed to keep the jazz scene going as a minority interest.

Years later the author, and some of our local jazz musicians were able to play with several of the band, including Kenny Ball, at various events in the area, but sadly not in Dunstable.

KENNY BALL AND HIS JAZZ BAND IN DUNSTABLE 1962

The occasion was the Priory Church summer Garden Fete in Priory Gardens in August 1962. The band was set up just inside the main gate from High St. South. The line-up was: Vic Pitt (Bass), John Bennett (Trombone), Kenny Ball (Trumpet), Dave Jones (Clarinet), Ron Bowden (Drums), Paddy Lightfoot (Banjo).

The Wayfarers Jazz Band at AC-Delco in the 1950s

From the mid 1950s to the early 1970s, the band played their brand of Dixieland jazz at various venues in Dunstable & district. They practiced for many years in the loft behind what was the 'Wagon & Horses' in High Street South (now called the 'Froth & Elbow'). Many friends and jazz fans regularly used to turn up and it became well known as a sort of jazz club for many years.

THE WAYFARERS JAZZ BAND AT AC-DELCO IN THE 1950s

The 'Wayfarers' at the old AC-Delco canteen at a New Year's Eve dance in the 1950s. L–R: Jim Collins, trombone; Paul Heley, trumpet; Harry Cadwell, drums; Tony Ward, clarinet; Fred Long, bass; Mike Stone, piano; Pete Hewson, guitar.

The Band also played for about fifteen years during the '50s, '60s, and early '70s at the monthly dances held by the (Old) Dunstablians Rugby Club, in the function room at the rear of the 'Old Sugar Loaf' Hotel in High Street North. The Rugby Club did not then have their own premises and used the 'Loaf' as a sort of clubhouse cum bar, before moving firstly to Bull Pond Lane, then to Thorn (near Houghton Regis).

The Band continued through the '70s & '80s, often appearing at dances at the Queensway Hall, then going back to their jazz roots in the 1990s but still playing locally in the new millennium, with a range of guests and personnel, and with several of the original 'Wayfarers' still involved.

THE WAYFARERS JAZZ BAND AT THE 'SUGAR LOAF' IN THE 1960s

The Band at a monthly O.D's Rugby Club Dance at the 'Old Sugar Loaf' in the 1960s – with a view of the dancers (below).

The line-up is:
Jim Collins – Trombone
Paul Heley – Trumpet
Tony Ward – Clarinet
Mike Stone – Piano and Banjo
Barry Potts – Bass
Dick Jeakins – Drums

THE WAYFARERS JAZZ BAND IN 1967

The Band is seen here pictured out of town at the *Rothamsted Research Centre* in Harpenden. The photo was taken at a dinner dance held at the Manor House in December 1967. Rothamsted was an historic building now being used as an Agricultural Research Centre. The band is seen in front of the ornate fireplace in the Main Hall. By this time Paul Heley had left to pursue his career studies and was replaced by Brian Jones on trumpet. Fred Long's place was taken by (Dr.) Mike Parker on bass; George Wallace had come in on drums for Harry ('H') Cadwell; Cliff Knott was now on guitar, with Tony Ward – clarinet, Mike Stone – piano, and Jim Collins – trombone, remaining from the original band.

Although personnel changes had occurred, the band continued playing at the (Old) Dunstablians Rugby Club dances etc. with the line-up above remaining for some time, and still essentially a jazz band, its more dance band role was yet to come in the nineteen seventies, when jazz became overwhelmed somewhat by the 'Pop' scene, and the band decided to play more 'commercial' music, while still retaining their jazz specialisation, until returning to their jazz roots in the mid 1980s. Paul Heley was later to return to the jazz scene after retiring in the late 1990s.

THE WAYFARERS JAZZ BAND AT 'THE ANGEL' TODDINGTON 1985

Above: L–R: Chris Reid, trombone; Brian Jones, trumpet; Tony Ward, clarinet.

Above: L–R: Chris Reid, trombone; Brian Jones, trumpet; Tony Ward, clarinet; Ken de Silva, drums; Phil Woodward, bass; Mike Stone, piano.
Guests included George Chisholm trombone, & John Denman clarinet.

Bagshawe's Modern Jazz Club in Dunstable in the 1960s

Below is a collage of many photographs taken at the Bagshawe's modern jazz club which flourished in the 1950s/60s. The organiser(s) managed to obtain the services of a succession of top British jazz musicians who were accompanied by the 'house band', a local trio comprising piano, bass, and drums.

THE BAGSHAWE'S COLLAGE

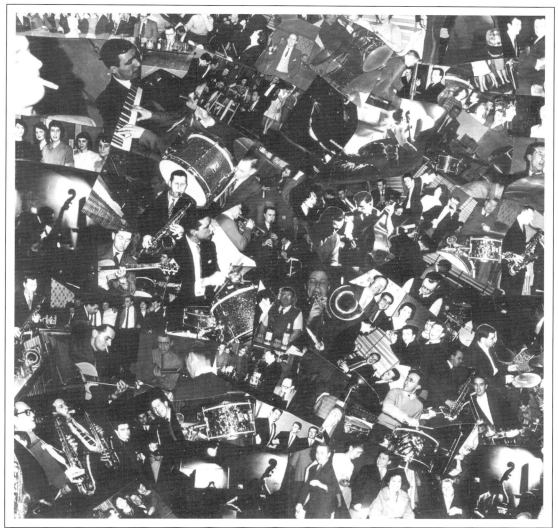

The collage was put together by drummer Alan Higgs (2nd top left), and re-photographed, and shows over one hundred musicians and fans.

Musicians in the Bagshawe's collage include: Bill Harris, piano; Alan Higgs, drums; John Wallwork, guitar; Stuart Horne, piano and sax; Paul Heley, trumpet; Tony Ward, clarinet; Mike Stone, bass, guitar, banjo; Harry Cadwell, drums; Don Rendell, Tenor Sax; Jim Collins, trombone; Cecil Boffin, guitar; Jackie Morrison, alto sax; M.Horton, bass. Some of the professional jazz musicians who guested over the years included: Don Rendell, tenor sax; Bill le Sage, vibes and piano; Bert Courtly, trumpet.

SOME OF THE PLAYERS IN THE BAGSHAWE'S COLLAGE

The Bagshawe's 'House Trio' was led on piano by Bill Harris, above right, from Dunstable, well known as a top class pianist in the jazz and dance band spheres. He was pianist with the 'Embassy' Dance Band for probably the whole of its existence and was always in demand to provide the high standards expected by the top jazz stars appearing at the club and elsewhere. (This picture was actually taken at the 'Old Sugar Loaf' in the 1950s and shows; John (Wally) Wallwork – guitar, Mike Stone – bass, Ken de Silva – drums, who played regularly at Bagshawe's). Many other local jazz musicians also regularly took part. The club was run by Alan Higgs & Peter Cole in Bagshawe & Co.'s canteen-social club building and attracted large numbers of the public to its sessions, as well as visiting musicians who often 'sat in'.

After Bagshawe's came to an end in 1960, the club had been invited to move to the Tulip Room (downstairs at the Halfway House). The jazz club continued there for some time, before finally closing in the early sixties.

The photographs opposite show (left to right): John Wallwork (Guitar), Don Rendell (Tenor Sax), Bill Harris (Piano), Lawrence Jeffs (Bass), Stuart Horne & Jackie Morrison (Alto Saxes), Paul Heley (Trumpet), Tony Ward (Clarinet), Lawrence Jeffs (small insert), Alan Higgs, Stuart Horne, Barry Potts, Mike Stone, John Wallwork, Bill Harris, Alan Higgs (below left), with Tony Ward, A. Higgs & Les Wood (also a regular Drummer there) sharing a small lemonade at the bar of the Tulip Room.

BAGSHAWE'S AND THE TULIP ROOM c.1960

BAGSHAWE'S AND THE HALFWAY HOUSE BALLROOM

Another regular musician at Bagshawe's was Mr. Rory McInnes, a tenor saxophonist from Luton, pictured left with members of the 'House' band.

The photo below shows a quartet playing for dancing upstairs in the popular Halfway House Ballroom, a busy venue for dinner-dances in those days. Taken in 1960, it shows Lloyd Connett, Bass, Alan Higgs, Drums, Bill Seaford, Piano, and an accordionist from St. Albans as yet un-named.

(All these photographs are from Alan Higgs' collection.)

DUNSTABLE

CELEBRATIONS

1963

THE PRIORY CHURCH 750TH ANNIVERSARY

The Programme of Events to be held at the Priory in 1963 set out the schedule of celebrations for the whole year. This included the week of the Pageant in June, which was to be organised by the Priory Church and the Town Council combined, and performed in Priory Gardens with the ancient Priory as the main backdrop. The events in the Priory's own particular programme were of course all related to the celebrations to be held at the Church throughout the year to mark the 750th anniversary of the founding of the Priory in 1213 A.D. (Building had started some 80 years before). It incorporated many musical performances, as listed below.

PRIORY MUSIC-FESTIVAL 1963

2nd Feb. St. Albans Abbey Choir – Recital.

16th Feb Charles Pope String Orchestra Concert

16th Mar Organ Recital by Dr. Arthur Wills (Ely)

15th May Organ Recital by Alan Wicks (Canterbury)

25th May Festival of Choirs

8th June Concert by the Renaissance Singers

24th June–29th June – THE PAGEANT

11th Sept Organ Recital by Peter Hurford (St. Albans)

18th Oct 750th Anniversary of the Priory

10th Dec The Messiah – performed by Luton Choral Society

The usual weekly and annual services took place, with the other special events featuring guest speakers, celebrities, Bishops and former Priory incumbents.

THE PRIORY SOUVENIR PROGRAMME

1213—1963

DUNSTABLE PRIORY · BEDFORDSHIRE

This was the cover of the Souvenir Programme (price 2/6d)which listed special events over the whole of 1963, including the Pageant of Dunstable to be held from 24th to 29th June in that year.

18 THE DUNSTABLE TOWN PAGEANT

The performance in June 1963 of the 'Pageant of Dunstable' reminded us of the story of Dunstable through the ages. The Pageant celebrated the beginnings of the town, the 750th anniversary of the founding of the Priory Church, and the 100th anniversary of the granting of Borough status in the Charter of 1864.

A SCENE FROM THE PAGEANT DURING A TOURNAMENT PROCESSION

(AW)

Photographs, tapes of the narrative and music, 8mm films, and a video transcript of the Pageant survive; a 25th anniversary exhibition was held in the library in 1988. It is a notable feature of the Pageant that no band or orchestra from Dunstable was available to perform in 1963 – those that had existed were defunct by that time. The organisers, the Town Council & the Priory Church, looked to the thriving Heath & Reach Brass Band to play in the production.

The Pageant was produced every evening from 24th–29th June 1963. While June has the longest days and the week included midsummer's day, nevertheless the later scenes often took place in low light and the weather was not always at its best, as can be seen from the photographs on the following page.

SCENES FROM THE PAGEANT

(AW

Tournament – Tilting scene. Knights charge with their lances at the lion figure on the left of the revolving arm.

(AW

A procession passes the Stage, probably in the Henry VIII annulment episode.

The National Press features The Pageant

One national paper actually ran a full broadsheet page of photographs with an article reporting the opening of the Pageant by the Duchess of Gloucester and explaining the background to the event, with pictures of the Duchess, with the Mayor, Mr M. Kilby, a section of the audience, and Saxon women cheering in the Foundation scene.

In 1963 Dunstable still possessed a large Printing industry base, Waterlow & Sons, Index Publishers, and one or two smaller businesses – enough for Dunstable College to run a dedicated Printing Department. The leaflet shown opposite was prepared by printing industry students at the College, and was overseen by a representative of the printing firms. The marks written on the draft are corrections requiring the attention of the students. The top illustration shows the front and back pages of the document. The lower one, the inner two pages. The leaflet provided a potted history of Dunstable – and an outline coverage of the Pageant, listing the eleven episodes.

PAGEANT 1963 ADVERTISING LEAFLET – DUNSTABLE COLLEGE

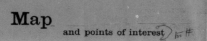

Map and points of interest

Key: 1. Priory Church   2. School   3. Town Hall   4-8. Car Parks

Already many people are hard at work, under the direction of Dorian Williams, Esq., M.F.H., making preparations for this great undertaking and, indeed, it is a great undertaking. Stands to seat 2,000 people will be erected and there will be public performances every evening at 8 p.m. from Monday, 24th June to Saturday, 29th June, with a matinee at 3 p.m. on Saturday afternoon. The Pageant has already aroused much interest in Bedfordshire, Hertfordshire and beyond and, if all goes well, the Pageant may well be a not unworthy contribution to the town's long history.

Admission prices for seats : 5s., 10s., 15s. and £1 (reduced prices for parties of 20 and above). Box Office opens May 1st at Chew's House, High Street South, Dunstable. Open 10 a.m. to 1 p.m. and 2 p.m. to 5 p.m., Monday to Saturday. Telephone 61507.

Ample car and coach parking   Light refreshments available

Produced as an exercise by students of the Department of Printing, College of Further Education, Dunstable

DUNSTABLE PAGEANT 24TH - 29TH JUNE

24·29 June   Dunstable Pageant 1963

In the year 1213, in the reign of King John, a vast gathering of people assembled in Dunstable for the consecration of the Priory Church of St. Peter by Hugh, Bishop of Lincoln. It was a great event for Dunstable, one of the greatest in its history which covers the space of over 2000 years.

Before the Romans came people lived and worked within the shadow of the Chiltern Hills, and through the centuries sat the centre of the town at the crossing of Watling Street and the ancient Icknield Way.

Kings, Queens and the great men of the land have passed this way. Henry I came to give protection from the 'robbers and beasts' who infested the town ; Queen Eleanor's funeral procession passed through the town and her body rested overnight in the Priory Church ; Edward III and Queen Philippa came to preside over a mediaeval tournament ; and the last sad moments of Henry VIII's divorce from his first wife were played out in the Priory Church.

The Civil War brought trouble to Dunstable, and the Minister was shot at in the pulpit. Then came the age of coaches and for a time prosperity returned. The ebb and flow of life through the centuries have brought many changes to the town, and in this century changes have moved more swiftly than before. The popu-

lation of this town has grown from 5,149 in 1901 to more than 25,000 today. The Mayor and Corporation appointed as the result of the charter granted to the town in 1864, now have a much greater population to care for, and to collect taxes from, than their predecessors of a century ago.

To celebrate the great event of 1213 and to remember with pride Queen Victoria's Charter of 1864 the town are combining to present in June 1963 a Pageant of Dunstable. On the green meadows of the Priory Church will be enacted once again some of the great events of its long history. The Dedication of the Priory, the great tournament of 1341 with jousting and all the colour and pageantry of the Middle Ages, the turmoil of the Civil War, and other scenes from the town's history portrayed by a thousand performers, promises to be a splendid and impressive spectacle.

The performance will consist of the following :

Prologue.
Romans and Ancient Britons Building of Watling Street and Icknield Way. Beginning of small community.

Episodes :
1. Play of St. Katherine, 1110
2. Founding of Town - Dunn the Robber, c. 1123
3. Dedication of Priory, 1213
4. Church versus Town, 1228
5. Eleanor's Funeral Procession, 1290
6. Tournament - including team of Archers - Edward III and Queen Philippa's visit in 1341
7. Henry VIII - Caterina of Aragon. Divorce Proceedings
8. A Puritan stronghold
9. Coach and Four - Moll Flanders
10. The Town Charter, 1864
11. The Age of Progress - Story up to date

Epilogue.
All performers to appear

A.D. 1110   1123   1213   1228   1290   1341   1533   1644   1864

The Pageant Programme June 1963

A 65-page Souvenir Programme was produced, covering all aspects of the event, with contributions from all the leading figures in its production. As well as information about the project, it contained the complete script for each episode, historical notes about Dunstable by Alec Fowler, and a full list of those

THE FRONT COVER OF THE SOUVENIR PROGRAMME

taking part in each episode, as well as the music selected (qv).

Each episode was titled according to the main topic to be covered, with either the specific date of the event featured shown in brackets or the range of years covered.

Every episode was accompanied by a selection of music deemed to be either of its era, or appropriate to its era. Except for the Fanfares, the Pageant Hymn, & the Heath Band (heard in episode eleven) which was taped separately (live) by Douglas Darby, the music was tape recorded from LP records (see later page). All the music, including the introductory ballads by the Ballad Singer, was mixed with the spoken dialogue and sound effects, then transferred to the Sound Track Tape. Each episode was then rehearsed, and performed to its own pre-recorded sound track. The tapes of the Pageant were carefully stored by Douglas Darby, and have been transcribed to digital mini-disc for safety.

THE EPISODES PERFORMED IN THE PAGEANT

Synopsis

PROLOGUE

Episode One	THE PLAY OF ST. CATHARINE (1110)	Seventeen
Episode Two	KING HENRY FOUNDS THE TOWN (1123)	Twenty Three
Episode Three	THE CONSECRATION OF THE PRIORY (18th OCTOBER 1213)	Twenty Seven
Episode Four	THE TOWN AGAINST THE PRIORY (1247)	Twenty Nine
Episode Five	QUEEN ELEANOR'S FUNERAL PROCESSION (1290)	Thirty Three
Episode Six	THE TOURNAMENT (1341)	Thirty Five
Episode Seven	THE DIVORCE OF KING HENRY VIIIth AND CATHERINE OF ARAGON (1533)	Thirty Nine
Episode Eight	THE CAVALIER RAID (1644)	Forty Five
Episode Nine	COUNTRY LIFE (1742)	Forty Seven
Episode Ten	THE CHARTER (1864)	Forty Nine
Episode Eleven	A CENTURY OF PROGRESS (1864-1963)	Fifty Three

EPILOGUE

THE MUSIC FOR THE PAGEANT – AS SELECTED FOR EACH EPISODE

Music of the Pageant

The music forms a very real part of the Pageant and its purpose is to adorn the story and create and deepen atmosphere. In choosing the music this has been the all important fact—that the music must be suitable to create and sustain atmosphere. But also, music used by the players in any episode must be drawn from that period and so in episodes 3, 5, 9 and 11 music has been taken as far as possible from sources contemporary with the incidents.

The Fanfares and the Pageant Hymn music have been specially written by local musicians.

The gathering and selection of music for a pageant such as this is no light task and has presented many problems— in the solving of which I acknowledge with gratitude the assistance of Mr. Robin Black, music master of Dunstable Grammar School, and Miss B. Cox and Mr. H. Hammond of Luton Music Library for their help and patience. Our thanks are due to Mr. F. M. Gardner, F.L.A., the Luton Borough Librarian for his permission to use the Music Library and to borrow from their extensive collection of records.

Our aim has been the deepening of atmosphere and the adornment of the story and I trust the music of the Pageant may help many to re-live parts of the history of this town and its ancient Priory Church.

RUPERT H. CHILD

Episode 1	Symphony No. 4 in B flat	*Beethoven*
Episode 2	Overture "William Tell"	*Rossini*
	English Dances	*Arnold*
	English Dance Tunes of 13th Century	
Episode 3	Psalm 122 (I was glad . . .)	*Plainsong (Tune VII)*
	Litany of the Saints	*Plainsong*
	Te-Deum	*Ambrosian Melody*
	Psalm 138 (I will give thanks . . .)	*Plainsong (VII)*
Episode 4	Promenade (from "Pictures at an exhibition")	*Mussorgsky*
	Great gate of Kiev (from "Pictures at an exhibition")	*Mussorgsky*
	Capriol suite (pavane)	*Warlock*
Episode 5	Agnus Dei trope "Crimina tollis, aspera mollis"	*13th Century Spanish Manuscript*
	Conductus "Quis dabit capiti meo"	*13th Century Spanish Manuscript*
Episode 6	Ein Heldenleben (Hero's life)	*Strauss*
Episode 7	Audivi Vocem	*Tallis*
Episode 8	"Storm" (from Scheherazade)	*Rimsky Korsakov*
Episode 9	Country Dances	*Arnold*
	St. Paul Suite	*Holst*
	English Folk Song Suite	*Vaughan Williams*
	Nell Gwyn Suite	*German*
Episode 10	"Jupiter" (from Planet Suite)	*Holst*
	March	
Episode 11	Invitation to the Dance	*Webber*
	Waltz—Blue Danube	*Strauss*
	Polka—Tristch Trastch	*Strauss*
	March Orb and Sceptre	*Walton*
	Grand March from "Aida"	*Verdi*
	Music linking the episodes	
	The Planet Suite	*Holst*
	Fanfares	composed by E. G. Hopkins
	Music for Pageant Hymn	composed by C. H. Scarf
		(Organist of Dunstable Priory)

The introductory paragraphs to the music programme of the pageant by the 'Balladeer', the Rev. Rupert Child, indicate the degree of effort that went into the provision of the Pageant's music.

EPISODES 9 AND 11 OF THE PAGEANT – 1742 AND 1864

The coaching Era in 1742 was featured in episode nine.

The Victorian era was the subject of the final episode (eleven), with particular emphasis on the achievement of obtaining Borough status in 1864.

(DTC)

PAGEANT 1963 – MUSIC AT THE CALIFORNIA BALLROOM

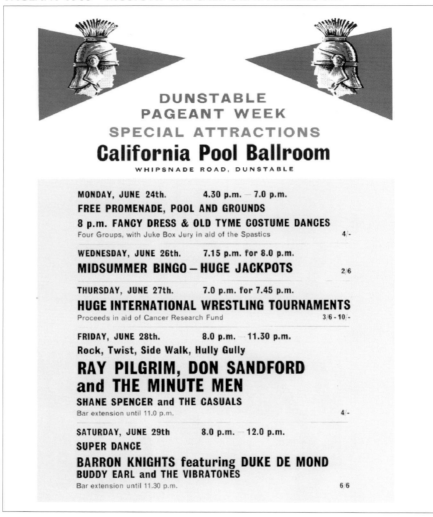

In 1963 The California Pool Ballroom was a comparatively new venue for Dunstable. This was an advertisement in the Pageant Programme, presenting their attractions during Pageant Week, and features the Pageant logo of a Roman Soldier's Head. The old outdoor swimming pool was still there, and many top names of the day were featured in the ballroom, as well as local groups.

PAGEANT PROGRAMME – ADVERTISERS INDEX

Index to Advertisers

Printed by The Leagrave Press Ltd. Luton and London

The list includes several once-thriving firms that are no longer in the town.

The Queensway Hall 1964–2001

This distinctive building was opened as the 'Civic Hall', by the Lord Mayor of London, Sir James Harman, on the 16th of April 1964, although from the following year it was to become known as the 'Queensway Hall'. It was a landmark feature of Dunstable for over 30 years, dominating the north-eastern quadrant of the town centre area with its unique architecture. Below, an early photograph mainly of the southern aspect of the Hall, showing the principal entrances, with the 'Quadrant' sculpture seen to the right.

(MM

It was designed to be a centre for the Arts, conferences etc. and for hire by local and outside organisations for a range of functions including dinner dances, shows etc, using the main hall and the areas around, with a council committee room and other areas upstairs.

As a result of the success of the Pageant of Dunstable in 1963, and the building of the hall in 1964, the Rev. H. Child and Mr. H.W. Parrott organised the revival of the Dunstable Amateur Operatic & Dramatic Society, (DAODS) to take advantage of these new modern facilities. The hall was to become home to many of their productions, and others, over the years.

All the leading bands played there, including The Glenn Miller Band, Joe Loss, Syd Lawrence and Ray McVay. There were many celebrity concerts featuring such artists as R.E.M., David Bowie, Blondie and Little Richard, plus top brass and military bands such as the Brighouse and Rastrick and the Black Dyke Mills Bands.

Eventually, due to various factors and reduced usage, (the DAODS also having

REVEREND R. H. CHILD, THE BALLAD SINGER

transferred to other venues), the hall was finally closed in 2001 and demolished. The site is now occupied by the ASDA store. At the time of writing, the District Council's plans for facilities to replace the Hall are well advanced and the town and district eagerly await the eventual completion of the new scheme.

DUNSTABLE

UPPER SCHOOLS

BANDS

AND

ORCHESTRAS

Dunstable's Upper Schools Music

This chapter includes reviews of the histories of music in the three Senior Dunstable Schools. Each of the schools will be known to the public in Dunstable through their appearances at the Grove House Gardens Performance Area and elsewhere.

The author and publisher are grateful to the Head Teachers and their dedicated music staff below, for providing the material for this section.

Manshead Upper School

Head Teacher – Mr. Ian Greenley
Head of Music – Mrs. Phyllida Driver

Northfields School (now Northfields College of Technology)

Head Teacher – Mr. Maclellan
Head of Music – Mr. Daggett (who took over from Mr Jonathan Mardlin from September 2002)

Queensbury School (now Queensbury College of Technology)

Head Teacher – Mr. R. Clayton (left Dec.2002)
Head of Music – Mr. Fred Thomas (retired in July 2002)
Mrs. Jane Thompson (from Summer 2002)

The Manshead School section covers the period 1978 to 2002, Northfields section covers the period from its inception in 1936 up to 2002, and the Queensbury section from 1991 to 2002.

19 MANSHEAD SCHOOL

History & Development of the Band & Orchestra

Manshead Upper School became the successor to the former Dunstable Grammar School for boys in 1975 under the then headmaster Mr.P.Banfield. The school has not so far possessed a definitive history as such of its musical faculties, history and development. However, music has been a strong feature at the school since its move from the Grammar School premises in High Street North to the mixed school campus at Caddington Turn.

Mrs Phyllida Driver has been the Head of Music for some years and has provided the bulk of the material for this chapter, including a selection of photographs, newspaper cuttings and her own recollections. She has identified 1978 as the year which most likely saw the introduction by the then Head of Music, Mr. Allun Jones, of instrumental and other music on a scale which has led to the development of the extensive musical groups that have continued to this day.

Mrs. Driver mentions an early foreign tour of Valkenburg in Holland in 1980–1981, which could possibly be the first of what has now become a tradition of musical exchanges, continental connections and tours by the school. By 1981, an exchange had also been established with the Lessing Gymnasium in Porz, Germany. The Band also played as a unit, with Allun Jones, in the Porz annual Carnival Procession. Not surprisingly perhaps the Band visited South Wales in 1983–1984 under the aegis of Mr. Jones. By 1985 however, Allun Jones had left, and Phyllida Driver inherited the facilities and traditions he had introduced, the Band, the Orchestra, the Choir, various small groups and the overseas connections. The size of the Band has varied from twenty-five players to fifty or so over the years, with the ages ranging from thirteen years, year nine, to eighteen years in the upper sixth form. Pupils often play in more than one group, and sing in the choir as well. The school stages annual full-scale musical productions which have included 'Kiss Me Kate', 'Godspell' & 'West Side Story'.

Until 1999 the school held regular 'Band Days' where pupils from other schools and other individuals joined in a day of rehearsals, with a concert in the

THE BADGE OF THE MANSHEAD SCHOOL BAND

Allun Jones was also responsible for the design of the Band's badge & logo. A close look at the badge shows a gold or yellow legend on the jersey's blue background, and reveals not only the detail of the french horn in the centre, and of course the title of the Band, but also a lower section of treble stave in black, completing the circle. An even closer look reveals that the music thereon comprises the opening bars of 'Land of my Fathers', both from left to right, and right to left!

evening. These were organised by Mr. Kevin Nicholls, a peripatetic brass teacher widely known in the area. It is hoped to have re-introduced this popular event in March 2003. From time to time, pupils are joined in concerts and activities by staff, parents and others who have supported the music of the school, among whom the names of Davina Owen, Liz Higgins, Jon Mardlin and Chris Cox have been mentioned.

THE BAND AT EATON BRAY CARNIVAL JULY 1990

Picture from the Dunstable Gazette July 11th 1990

Members of the school Concert Band are seen here playing at the Eaton Bray Carnival, perched on the back of a large lorry – though whether they are moving or not at this point is not clear. Four clarinets and four flutes are in evidence with other players seated behind. There must also have been electric power available to drive the electric keyboard. The drummer can be seen behind the pianist, with no doubt a bass to the back of the vehicle. Boaters are either being worn or placed under the seat. (It is not particularly easy playing on a moving vehicle with stops and starts!)

The school continues to flourish in its musical activities and many individual pupils have gone on to higher things. At the time of writing, in 2002, a group from the school had recently performed outside the Priory Church at its July summer fete, after an appearance by the Band at a Concert in the Park in Grove House Gardens the previous Sunday.

The chapter includes a selection of photos from a range of musical activities in this country and abroad. Some of the largest group photographs have proved a little too large for inclusion, but the pictures chosen are representative of the school and its remarkable range of activities. The children are fortunate that under its Headmaster Mr. Ian Greenley and staff led by Mrs. Driver, the school continues to provide a wide ranging musical education for its pupils.

MANSHEAD SCHOOL BAND IN THE PARKS

Above – Wardown Park Luton, summer 1990.   Below – Priory Gardens Dunstable, summer 1992.

THE ORCHESTRA 'ON THE ROAD' AND 'AT HOME'

Above: Porz – Germany, exchange trip – Carnival & Concert.

A small ensemble at Westways Old People's Residence, Dunstable.

THE BAND ON TOUR IN GERMANY IN 1992

Above: The Manshead School Band/Orchestra during February 1992, the backdrop emphasising the wintry season.

Left: Another scene from a tour of Germany.

The School considers it is important to maintain the tradition of touring abroad, and this tour seems to be enjoyed by the pupils as evidenced by their smiles in the winter sunshine.

BAND GROUP PHOTO – NOVEMBER 1994

ORCHESTRA PHOTO – NOVEMBER 1994

'KISS ME KATE' IN MARCH 1995

The School production of 'Kiss Me Kate' in this Gazette photo featured Claire de Silva as Lilli Vanessi, with Jeremy Cladd, Lisa Barton and the full company. The Producer was Sarah Fitzsimmons, Musical Director, Phyllida Driver.

CHRISTMAS 1995

The Band plays at the Wyevale Garden Centre, Caddington. Father Christmas was due to appear by helicopter and motorcycle.

1999 – WITH GUESTS FROM OTHER SCHOOLS

THE PRIORY AND GROVE HOUSE

The Concert Band at one of the Town Council's 'Concerts in the Park' in Priory Gardens in the summer of 1991.

A-Level students at a Tuesday lunchtime concert in the Dunstable Town Council Committee Room at Grove House in the year 2001.

(AW)

Head of Music Mrs. Phyllida Driver conducts a contingent of the Orchestra outside the Priory Church at the Church Fete in July 2002.

(AW)

The school orchestra in Grove House Gardens in the Sunday Summer Bands Programme of 2002, under the baton of Mr. Chris Cox.

AT GLENWOOD SCHOOL

A Manshead School group is pictured above playing for the young people at Glenwood School, an example of the charity performances carried out by the school and the sense of community achieved thereby.

Nowadays, school bands do not often march in parades and 'firemen's galas' as did the Excelsior of old, (apart from the occasional carnival in Germany), and of course the age range is centred on school pupils of senior age groups and not the general public.

In contrast to the old bands though, many schools nowadays travel and play abroad and open department stores amongst other things, and many individuals do later become involved in other musical groups and activities, having had a good grounding in their schools' musical activities and training. We must hope that these traditions and standards will continue and not fall prey to pressures on education budgets.

20 NORTHFIELDS SCHOOL

Northfields School Bands – History and Development

Northfields Upper School was originally founded in January 1936, opening on the 13th January as the Northfields Senior Elementary School, with Mr. F. A. Underwood as headmaster and Miss K. W. Rutt as music teacher. She was to leave in 1938 after two years or so having set up a school choir.

All this, and most of the other information on the school and its music up to 1986, comes from a book published in 1986, written by Mr. K.Keates, member of staff 1947–1980 & second master from 1961. His book, entitled 'Northfields School 1936–1986' was produced with thanks and acknowledgements to the headmaster, pupils, the Dunstable Gazette, Dunstable public library and the Town Council, to mark the school's Jubilee 1936–1986.

Some of the musical references in the book include the following:

1939 – A wireless set and gramophone were purchased.

1951 – Mr. R. Warwick succeeded Mr. Erskine Page as director of music.

1951 – Eisteddfod in the Town Hall, under Mr. Warwick assisted by Mr. G.Bass (piano), and later a programme of music and dance including a 'Pageant of Dunstable'.

1952 – A choral concert accompanied on the piano by Mr.Bass (Art & Music), who also played weekly recitals during assembly.

1961 – The beginnings of a brass band by Mr. D. Boundy (Woodwork), with the headmaster Mr. Langley joining in. It was also noted that in early days Mr. A. Bavister of the Salvation Army performed 'wind solos' at speech days.

1964 – May, the school was part of a choral performance at the 'Civic Hall'.

1976 – The school band run by Miss Barrett had been playing since 1967 and now had 22 members in the 13 to 18 years age group.
– The Band of the Royal Marines came to the school and the bands rehearsed together. (Nigel Patten at 14 years of age conducted the Marines Band).

1978 – 'Billy Liar' was produced.
– In June Mr. Willoughby and Mrs. Henson accompanied 24 pupils on a musical exchange with Le Quenevais School, Jersey.

1979 – Teachers at the school produced and took part in a 'rock-opera' entitled 'The Street', produced by Mr. T. McLaughlin.
– The school's Concert Band made a link with the Alesund Music School in Norway.
– Simon Capell (18) was chosen to play drums with a top star after being spotted at a performance of the school band at the Mayor's Ball.
– Thirty-nine members of the band combined with a Jersey band for a school concert.

1983 – George Chisholm played with the band at a concert in the school hall. In May, the school played host to the National Schools Band Association, with Bryan Willoughby as Musical Director.
– Mr. Keates' book also refers to a recent tour of Germany where the band was 'treated like Royalty'. They had been accompanied by Mr. Derek Bird

MUSIC

Northfields Band Association

Northfields School Band was formed in 1978. Since then it has grown in both size and widespread popularity. There are 40 members whose ages range from 13-18 years. Northfields Band is primarily a swing band, although they cover a wide range including jazz and popular music. The band is often called upon to play at major civic functions in and around Dunstable as well as giving illustrated lectures, concerts and television appearances. They have also held their own concert, discos and celebrity concerts with Don Lusher, Kenny Baker, and the Band's Honorary President George Chisholm. The annual band tour always proves highly successful, for many years Northfields Band has exchanged with Le Rocquier school band in Jersey.

In 1983 the band undertook its first foreign tour to Koblenz in West Germany where they were the first British band to play in the famous Phantasialand. The great success of this tour was surpassed only by the tour of Austria in 1984, where over 800 people turned out to the first concert.

The band had many bookings for 1985 including a TV appearance with George Chisholm, a show with Joe Loss, a summer tour in Jersey and a host of concerts.

In 1986, the year of Expo 86, the band hopes to go to Canada for their summer tour, and to help raise funds, the band have made their first album "Undecided".

Visits	**Concerts**
1982 Jersey	1982 Don Lusher
1983 Germany	1983 George Chisholm
1984 Austria	1984 Kenny Baker
1985 Jersey	1985 George Chisholm
1986 Vancouver (Canada)	

K. Keates' Book – Appendix

who spoke of a superb tour, with the players proving marvellous ambassadors for the school and their country. It was announced by Mr. Willoughby that the band was now giving some 30 concerts a year with £8,000 to £10,000 in running costs and that a second band had been formed to feed into the main one.

1984 – The Silver Jubilee of Twin Town arrangements was celebrated at the Queensway Hall, 400 attending. Music for dancing was supplied by the Band. Later in the year a fund raising event was held at the Queensway Hall. Members, parents and staff raised £600 for the Band's finances. A later concert helped to raise £400 towards medical equipment.

– The Band celebrated its developing status by producing a record entitled 'Undecided' which was launched by Jazz trombonist George Chisholm who praised the performance of the Band. This was part of a fund raising campaign to take the Band to Vancouver to take part in the 'Expo 86' World Trade Fair. £20,000 was raised. Concerts in the year included an appearance at RAF Halton.

1985 – Plans for the 'EXPO' Tour continued during the year.

1986 – Mr. Keates records the comments of the head girl in 1986, Sue Taylor, recalling celebrity concerts featuring Don Lusher, Kenny Baker and George Chisholm. Also, the Music & Drama's Dept productions of 'The Mikado', 'The Boyfriend', etc. and the improvements in facilities for music and drama. –Reference to the planned visit to Canada, due later in the year, ends the main part of Mr. Keates' book on the school. (An Appendix – 'Music'– summarises some of the highlights of the School band). The book of course covers the whole history of the School from 1936 to mid 1986 in the context of other social and educational developments locally and nationally, and is available in the School Library.

K. KEATES' BOOK – TWO VINTAGE PICTURES

Left, The first school band 1963.

Right, Patron Mr.George Chisholm with Band members, taken in 1984.

THE SWING BAND

THE 1980s

BRYAN WILLOUGHBY RECEIVES A VAUXHALL AWARD ON BEHALF OF THE BAND

(VM)

GEORGE CHISHOLM LEADS THE BAND AT A SCHOOL CONCERT

CELEBRITY CONCERT PROGRAMME 25TH MARCH 1983, PATRON GEORGE CHISHOLM

Grundfos Pumps
wish the
Northfield School Band
continued success for
1983

GRUNDFOS

Grundfos Pumps Ltd. Grovebury Road. Leighton Buzzard. Beds LU7 8TL
Tel: (0525) 374876 Telex: 825544

Northfields Band Association
presents

A CELEBRITY CONCERT
featuring

GEORGE CHISHOLM
with the

NORTHFIELDS SCHOOL BAND

FRIDAY 25th March, 1983 at 8.00 p.m.

Headmaster
D. FONE, B.Sc., F.R.G.S.   PROGRAMME 10p

GEORGE CHISHOLM

Welcome to our second 'Celebrity Concert', and to our guest this evening, Mr. George Chisholm. We are particularly grateful to him for agreeing to play this engagement as he is still 'officially' in his convalescence period following a major operation and we wish him well and hope that our work with him tonight will not cause any set back to his recovery!

George Chisholm was born in Glasgow, where he eventually started piano lessons and played for local children's concert troupes, and dances. He took up the trombone in 1934, moving to London in 1936, where he played in night-clubs until joining American bandleader Benny Carter in Holland for three months making records with that band, and Coleman Hawkins. He has also recorded with Fats Waller, and played with Louis Armstrong on several dates. He performed with the Ambrose orchestra from 1938 until joining the Royal Air Force, where the famous Squadronaires Dance Orchestra was formed. He stayed with them (playing alongside his good friend, and our guest last year, Don Lusher) until he joined the B.B.C. Show Band in 1950 for five years, during which time he took part in the Goon Show series. He was also with the Black and White Minstrel Show for five years. He has appeared as guest in such shows as the Billy Cotton Band Show, The John Junkin Show, The Golden Shot, The Good Old Days, The David Nixon Show, Val Doonican and many others including Morcambe and Wise. He free-lances in recording, T.V. and Radio dates together with numerous solo appearances in cabaret and jazz concerts. He had several group and solo records to his name, and is due to make three more L.P's. in the near future.

My thanks again to George Chisholm, and to you, the members of the audience, for your continued support. We have had a full programme of concerts again this year and I am sure you wish the Band a successful tour in Germany this coming July.

Bryan Willoughby.

MEMBERS OF THE BAND

FLUTES	TENOR SAXOPHONES
Kay Jackson	Caroline Bird(and Baritone)
Frances Sharp	Christopher Denton
Bryony Hicks	Jackie Foster
Wendy Nicolson	Tracey Butterfield
Alison Vermeer	TRUMPETS
Jeanette Carvisiglia	Donna Joy
Jeremy Musannif	Stephen Denton
Melanie Haile	Simon Stevens
Susan Taylor	Susan Ogley
OBOE	Kim Marsh
Emma Horstman	Bryony Hicks
CLARINETS	FRENCH HORNS
Melanie Thomas	Mary Jarrett
Jennifer Austing	Jeremy Hicks
Claire Bevan	EUPHONIUM
Sally Cavalier	John Whittall
Karen Smith	TROMBONES
Simon Musannif	Paul Jackson
Anne Bodsworth	Carolyn Hicks
Samantha Catlow	Kevin Taylor
Rachel Adams	Colin Richards
BASS CLARINET	Malcolm Patrick
Kerry Gilheany	KEYBOARD BASS
ALTO SAXOPHONES	Peter Cadigan
Anna Carvisiglia(and Baritone)	
Zoe Dent	RHYTHM GUITAR
Susan Nicolson	Jeff Poynter
Ellen Donaghy	PERCUSSION
Dawn Earwicker	Andrew Tournay
	Neil Valentine
	Ken Footitt

BACKING GROUP FOR GEORGE CHISHOLM

Nicky Burnham – Piano	Jeff Poynter – Guitar
Kevin Glee – Bass	Sam Catchlove – Drums
MUSICAL DIRECTOR	ASSISTANT MUSICAL DIRECTOR
Bryan Willoughby	Peter Cadigan

Above: Members of the Band, and a message from Bryan Willoughby.

FRIENDS OF THE BAND

Mr. and Mrs. J. Allen
Barclays Bank Ltd.
Mr. and Mrs. D.F. Bird
Mr. D. Braybrooks
Grunfos Pumps Ltd.
Mr. and Mrs. M.A. Hicks
Mr. and Mrs. P.J. Horstman
Mr. and Mrs. J. Jarrett
Mr. R.A. Lowther
National Westminister Bank Ltd.

* * * * * * * *

We are grateful to Grundfos Pumps Ltd. for their very generous sponsorship for this year's Band Tour to Germany.

* * * * * * *

FUTURE DATES

April 11th	8.00 p.m. Combined Concert with the Band of Le Rocquier School, Jersey, who recently appeared in the B.B.C. series 'BERGERAC'.
May 21st	National Association of School Bands Festival
May 30th	Dunstable Carnival
July 9th-17th	The Band will be on Tour in Germany.

NORTHFIELDS SCHOOL BAND IN CANADA AT 'EXPO 1986'

Above, Margaret Thatcher is seen speaking at EXPO '86 in Canada, with the Band in attendance.

Below, Bryan Willoughby and members of the Band are congratulated by the Prime Minister at EXPO '86.

BRYAN WILLOUGHBY CONDUCTS

Bryan Willoughby is seen here conducting a smaller ensemble, with the patron of the Band at the time, Mr. Keith Baldwin, on trumpet to the middle right of the picture. Keith Baldwin succeeded George Chisholm as patron some time after George's death in the late 1980s. Sadly, the untimely death of Bryan Willoughby was to occur a few years later.

Keith Baldwin, who for many years promoted jazz sessions at the 'Angel Inn', Toddington, and ran his own Big Band, eventually relinquished his patronage when he decided to move to Spain, where he continued his interest in band music.

THE BAND IN PRIORY GARDENS – c.1990

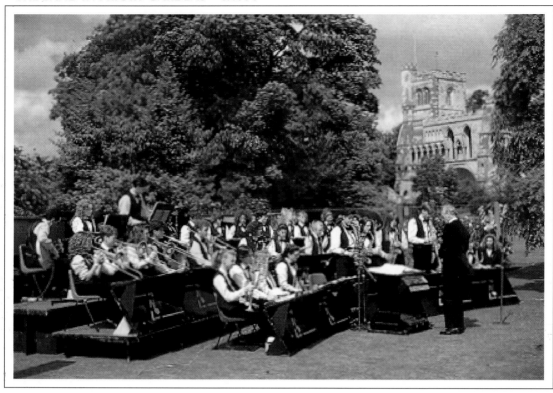

(D

This delightful picture appeared in Dunstable Town Council's Guide to Dunstable, with the Band seen against the backdrop of the Priory Church, when the summer Sunday afternoon concerts were still held in Priory Gardens. The setting was always an attractive one and provided a degree of intimacy with the public.

The Council was unable to build a permanent bandstand in Priory Gardens due to planning restrictions in force for this area. The concerts were later to transfer to the new Millennium Performance area in Grove House gardens from 2000 where the Northfields Band has since appeared.

NORTHFIELDS SCHOOL BAND – 2000

The Northfields School Band in The Gazette, *of 18th October 2000, pictured on their return from a British TV recording and a tour of Italy. ITV filmed the band performing and interviewed one of the teachers as part of a 'Stars in their Lives' documentary of 'Steps' star Faye Tozer, who was a member of the Northfields Band in her school days.*

21 QUEENSBURY SCHOOL

The Queensbury School Bands – Recent History

Queensbury High School was formed in the 1980s with the amalgamation of two former schools, Queen Eleanor's School for Girls and Kingsbury School, the new name being derived from both the schools' names. Each of the former schools would have had their own musical activities and the new school would have incorporated these traditions. However this chapter looks specifically at the period from the time the Queensbury Band was re-formed in 1991 by the then newly appointed Head of Music, Mr. Fred Thomas, up to his retirement in July 2002, (most of that period having been under the headmastership of Mr. R. Clayton). (Mr. Clayton has since become head of school improvement in Bedfordshire after eight and a half years at Queensbury).

Fred Thomas recalls that the musicians were split into two distinct groups, a Wind Band and a Jazz Band, in order to provide the widest possible variety of styles and performance. The two bands began performing regularly both in and out of school, and an annual music exchange was established with the Nicolaus Cusanus Gymnasium in Bergisch Gladbach near Cologne in Germany. Since then, musicians from both schools have benefited from playing together on many occasions, and the school bands go on bi-annual European music tours. The pictures on subsequent pages highlight this aspect in particular.

During this 11-year period, the Wind Band was conducted for a while in 1993 by Mr. David Stokes, the second music teacher, as featured in one of the photographs opposite.

Each musician in both bands has his or her own music stand and banner as well as the bands' definitive logo stands, all of which were designed and paid for by the Parent–Staff Association and include the original 'crown' logo of the School. As well as their overseas tours the bands have performed on many occasions locally at the school of course and at venues in Dunstable and district, including the summer concerts formerly in Priory Gardens and now Grove House Gardens. They have made other appearances including the South Beds. Show as a full band, also the Quadrant and other venues, with the Jazz Band undertaking a diverse number of engagements of its own. The Band played in the Quadrant in early December 2002.

The school has now acquired the status of College of Technology, and continues its musical traditions under its new Head of Music, Mrs. Jane Thompson.

Early days of the jazz band in 1991. On the second tenor sax is Mark Webb who was later to become the school's guitar teacher in the 2000s.

The Wind Band at a school concert in 1993, conducted by Mr. David Stokes, at the time the second music teacher.

HOLLAND 1994

Members of the Wind Band are pictured relaxing during their tour of Holland in 1994. Seated front row centre is the School's Head of Music, Mr. Fred Thomas.

The Band is seen performing at an old people's centre near Maastricht during their tour of Holland in 1994.

AUSTRIA 1996

The Band is here seen enjoying the sunshine on the terrace of the Spa Gardens in Aachen, displaying their logo – no doubt who they are and where they are from!

All smiles as the combined Bands and adults prepare to go down the salt mines in Austria in 1996. Perhaps they were working their passage on this tour!

AUSTRIA 1996

1996 and another photograph from the Austrian tour, taken at the Festival Hall in Alpendorf.

KONZERT
VON

Queensbury High School

Concert Band

aus England

Sonntag, den 30 Juni 1996

am Parkplatz vor der Kabinenbahn
(bei Schlechtwetter in der
Festhalle Alpendorf)

20.00 UHR

POPULARE REPERTOIRE *mit Musik von den*
sechsigen Jahren und Jazz

FREIER EINTRITT

Veranstalter: NST Music Tours

Left: a poster (somewhat reduced in scale) advertising the Band's appearance on 30th June 1996, in the 'Festhalle' in Alpendorf.

The Band has been captured here, playing on a bandstand at the appropriately named 'Phantasialand' (Germany's biggest leisure park) in the late 1990s.

Back home in England to play for the South Beds. Show in 1997.

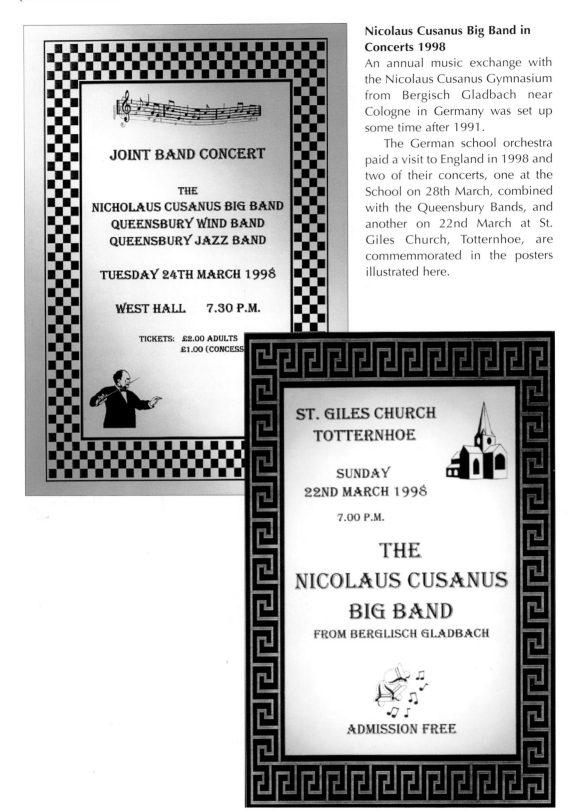

Nicolaus Cusanus Big Band in Concerts 1998

An annual music exchange with the Nicolaus Cusanus Gymnasium from Bergisch Gladbach near Cologne in Germany was set up some time after 1991.

The German school orchestra paid a visit to England in 1998 and two of their concerts, one at the School on 28th March, combined with the Queensbury Bands, and another on 22nd March at St. Giles Church, Totternhoe, are commemmorated in the posters illustrated here.

JOINT BAND CONCERT

THE

NICHOLAUS CUSANUS BIG BAND
QUEENSBURY WIND BAND
QUEENSBURY JAZZ BAND

TUESDAY 24TH MARCH 1998

WEST HALL   7.30 P.M.

TICKETS: £2.00 ADULTS
£1.00 (CONCESS

ST. GILES CHURCH
TOTTERNHOE

SUNDAY
22ND MARCH 1998

7.00 P.M.

THE

NICOLAUS CUSANUS

BIG BAND

FROM BERGLISCH GLADBACH

ADMISSION FREE

THE NICOLAUS CUSANUS BIG BAND IN DUNSTABLE, 2000 AND 2002

The photo above shows the Queensbury Band at home to the Nicolaus Cusanus Band from Germany, in a combined concert at the school in 2000. The audience appear well supplied with refreshments while enjoying listening to the music. Below, another close-up view of the members of both Bands in 2002.

HOLLAND 2000

This much-travelled Band is pictured in Holland in 2000, where they are seen playing at Noordwijk am Zee: Fred Thomas is wielding the baton.

The same year 2000, again in Holland, this time appearing at a venue in Valkenburg.

THE JAZZ BAND – CHRISTMAS FUND-RAISING CONCERT

Finally this picture, taken at the school, shows the Jazz Band helping to raise funds at a recent Christmas bazaar, with Fred Thomas conducting.

Postscript

This book has attempted to describe how the roles, repertoires, customs, technology and social circumstances have changed with respect to Brass Bands, Wind Bands, Orchestras and various other Groups, in celebrations and in music making in Dunstable and district over two centuries overall. It has concentrated on people in the town of Dunstable and around, who over the years have got together – (or who have been got together by leading enthusiasts) – to learn and play music (mainly for the public) in concerts, fetes, churches, carnivals, festivals and celebrations of a civic or public nature, and have provided the facilities for the training and development of young musicians.

Traditional music forms, and acoustic instruments and their development, have been the main features, although modern electronics make a useful contribution to all forms of music nowadays. The book does not include Pop or Rock groups and their particular performance venues – (being a separate, specialised area) – as this would require an archive of its own, though sharing a common history with much of the contents of the book.

Recent times have seen a good deal of the legacy of earlier years continued in the establishment of Brass and Wind Bands, Orchestras, small Groups and Choirs in our schools, with the Salvation Army Band still maintaining its traditions, and with choral groups, secular and church music and other groups continuing to keep going in spite of various setbacks from time to time.

The absence of a 'Town Band' as such in Dunstable, unlike some of the surrounding towns and villages, continues to be a cause of regret, but the recent history of, for example, the Toddington Town Band provides some cause for hope, and the summer Band Concerts series, alternating with the winter Recital programme, organised and supported by Dunstable Town Council, are very important factors at present in providing opportunities for Bands and individuals to play to the public, and for the citizens of the town to be entertained in pleasant surroundings. Also, at the time of writing, plans for the replacement facilities for the much missed Queensway Hall are in the later stages of development, and we all have high hopes for Music and the Arts in Dunstable and district in the future.